C++ for Game Developers: Building Scalable and Robust Gaming Applications

JARREL E.

In the realm of pixels and polygons, where
creativity meets code, C++ stands as the archi-
tect's language, crafting worlds of wonder and
challenges for those who dare to play.

Jarrel E.

Contents

Foreword

C++ for Game Developers: Building Scalable and Robust Gaming Applications is a transformative journey for individuals aspiring to navigate into the dynamic C++ game programming.

Upon contemplating the information presented in this book, the author's dedication to offering a thorough and comprehensible manual on C++ game creation strikes me. If you are an experienced developer looking to expand your knowledge base, this book is a great resource.

Preface

As an author passionate about both C++ programming and the immersive world of game development, it is my pleasure to present this comprehensive guide tailored for developers aspiring to create high-performance and resilient gaming applications.

Learning the nuances of the C++ programming language is an essential starting point for anyone interested in the fast-paced world of game creation, where efficiency and creativity are critical factors. This book is designed to be your guide as you progress toward becoming a skilled game developer. It offers a thorough understanding of C++ fundamentals as well as a plethora of knowledge on creating programs that scale well and withstand the demands of the gaming industry.

Acknowledgement

Gratitude to the vibrant community of C++ developers for their continuous contributions and support in shaping the landscape of game development. Appreciation for the C++ Standard Committee and the contributors to the C++ programming language, whose dedication has been instrumental in enhancing the tools available to game developers.

Special thanks to my fellow game developers who shared their insights, experiences, and expertise, enriching the content of this book. Recognition of the gaming industry pioneers whose innovative spirit has paved the way for new possibilities and challenges, inspiring the content of this book.

A sincere thank you to the technical reviewers whose meticulous feedback and suggestions have played a crucial role in ensuring the accuracy and quality of the material. Grateful acknowledgment to the editorial team for their commitment to excellence and their efforts in refining the manuscript to meet the highest standards.

Introduction to C++ in Game Development

Understanding the Fundamentals of C++

This chapter serves as a gateway to the world of C++ for aspiring game developers, providing a comprehensive overview of key concepts, syntax, memory management, and a glimpse into the realm of object-oriented programming (OOP). By mastering these fundamental aspects, you pave the way for robust and scalable game development.

Key Concepts and Syntax

Basics of C++

C++, an extension of the C programming language, brings a powerful set of features to the table. At its core, C++ combines procedural and object-oriented programming paradigms, offering a versatile toolkit for software development. Let's delve into some key concepts:

Variables and Data Types

In C++, variables serve as containers for storing data. The data type of a variable determines the kind of values it can hold. Here's a simple example:

```cpp
#include <iostream>

int main() {
    // Variable declaration and initialization
```

```cpp
    int playerScore = 100;

    // Displaying the value
    std::cout << "Player Score: " << playerScore << std::endl;

    return 0;
}
```

In this snippet, we declare an integer variable (**playerScore**) and assign it the value of 100. The **std::cout** is used for output, displaying the player's score on the console.

Control Flow

C++ provides various constructs for controlling the flow of a program, including **if** statements for conditional execution and loops such as **for** and **while** for repetitive tasks:

```cpp
#include <iostream>

int main() {
    int playerHealth = 75;

    // Conditional statement
    if (playerHealth > 0) {
        std::cout << "Player is still alive!" << std::endl;
    } else {
        std::cout << "Game over!" << std::endl;
    }

    // Looping example
    for (int i = 0; i < 5; ++i) {
        std::cout << "Iteration: " << i << std::endl;
    }

    return 0;
}
```

This snippet showcases an **if** statement for checking player health and a **for** loop iterating five times.

Functions

Functions encapsulate blocks of code, promoting modularity and reusability. Consider the following function:

```cpp
#include <iostream>

// Function declaration
void greetPlayer(const std::string& playerName) {
    std::cout << "Welcome, " << playerName << "!" << std::endl;
}

int main() {
    // Function call
    greetPlayer("Adventurer");

    return 0;
}
```

Here, we define a function **greetPlayer** that takes a **std::string** parameter. The function is then called within the **main** function.

Memory Management in C++

Efficient memory management is crucial in game development to ensure optimal performance and avoid memory leaks. C++ provides mechanisms for dynamic memory allocation and deallocation through **new** and **delete** operators:

```cpp
#include <iostream>

int main() {
    // Dynamic memory allocation
```

```cpp
    int* dynamicInt = new int;
    *dynamicInt = 42;

    // Displaying the dynamically allocated value
    std::cout << "Dynamic Integer: " << *dynamicInt << std::endl;

    // Dynamic memory deallocation
    delete dynamicInt;

    return 0;
}
```

In this example, we allocate memory for an integer using **new**, assign a value, and then free the memory with **delete** to prevent memory leaks.

A Sneak Peek into Object-Oriented Programming (OOP)

Object-oriented programming is a paradigm that organizes code around objects, combining data and functions that operate on that data. Let's explore a simple OOP concept: classes and objects.

Classes and Objects

A class is a blueprint for creating objects, defining their structure and behavior. Objects are instances of classes. Consider a basic example:

```cpp
#include <iostream>

// Class declaration
class Player {
public:
    // Member variable
    int health;

    // Member function
    void takeDamage(int damage) {
```

```cpp
        health -= damage;
        std::cout << "Player took " << damage << " damage.
        Remaining health: " << health << std::endl;
    }
};

int main() {
    // Creating an object of the Player class
    Player gamePlayer;

    // Initializing member variable
    gamePlayer.health = 100;

    // Calling member function
    gamePlayer.takeDamage(20);

    return 0;
}
```

Here, we defined a **Player** class with a member variable **health** and a member function **takeDamage**. In the **main** function, we create an object of the **Player** class, set its health, and invoke the **takeDamage** method.

Game Development Foundations

Essential Game Development Tools

Having a good collection of tools is essential when working in the dynamic field of C++ game development. This chapter examines the fundamental resources that enable game developers to produce engrossing and immersive experiences. From integrated development environments (IDEs) to version control systems, each tool plays a crucial role in streamlining the development process.

Integrated Development Environments (IDEs)

Visual Studio

Visual Studio stands as a stalwart in the world of C++ game development. Its feature-rich environment, seamless integration with compilers, and powerful debugging tools make it a preferred choice for many developers. Here's a snippet showcasing a simple C++ program in Visual Studio:

```cpp
#include <iostream>

int main() {
    std::cout << "Hello, Visual Studio!" << std::endl;
    return 0;
}
```

This basic program outputs a welcoming message to the console, highlighting the simplicity of getting started with Visual Studio.

Code::Blocks

Code::Blocks is an open-source IDE that offers a lightweight yet powerful platform for C++ development. With its customizable interface and support for multiple compilers, it provides flexibility to developers. Below is a snippet demonstrating a console-based C++ program in Code::Blocks:

```
#include <iostream>

int main() {
    std::cout << "Hello, Code::Blocks!" << std::endl;
    return 0;
}
```

This example mirrors the simplicity of the previous code but showcases the compatibility of Code::Blocks as an alternative IDE.

Version Control Systems

Git

Git is an indispensable tool for collaborative game development. Its distributed version control system allows developers to track changes, collaborate seamlessly, and manage different versions of the game code. Let's consider a basic scenario where Git is used to track changes in a C++ project:

```
# Initialize a Git repository
git init

# Add a C++ file to the repository
git add main.cpp

# Commit the changes
git commit -m "Initial commit: Hello World in C++"
```

This sequence of Git commands sets up a repository, adds a C++ file, and commits the changes with a descriptive message.

Build Systems

CMake

CMake simplifies the build process, enabling developers to generate platform-specific build files. Its cross-platform nature makes it an excellent choice for C++ game development. Consider a basic CMakeLists.txt file:

```
cmake_minimum_required(VERSION 3.10)
project(GameDevelopment)
set(CMAKE_CXX_STANDARD 14)
add_executable(Game main.cpp)
```

This CMakeLists.txt file defines a project named "GameDevelopment" with a C++ standard of 14 and an executable named "Game" from the source file main.cpp.

Debugging Tools

GDB (GNU Debugger)

GDB is a powerful debugger that aids in identifying and fixing issues in C++ code. It allows developers to set breakpoints, inspect variables, and step through the code. Here's a simple example:

```
# Compile the program with debugging information
g++ -g main.cpp -o my_program

# Start GDB
gdb my_program
```

```
# Set a breakpoint
break main

# Run the program
run
```

These commands demonstrate compiling a program with debugging information, starting GDB, setting a breakpoint at the main function, and running the program under GDB control.

Profiling Tools

Valgrind

Valgrind is a powerful tool for detecting memory leaks and profiling C++ code. Let's look at a scenario where Valgrind is used to check for memory leaks:

```
# Compile the program with debugging information
g++ -g main.cpp -o my_program

# Run Valgrind to check for memory leaks
valgrind --leak-check=full ./my_program
```

This snippet showcases compiling a program with debugging information and using Valgrind to identify and report any memory leaks.

Graphics and Visualization Tools

OpenGL Debugger (gldebug)

For game developers working with OpenGL, tools like gldebug provide insights into the graphics rendering process. Although it's not an exhaustive example, the following illustrates how gldebug might be used:

```cpp
#include <GL/gl.h>
#include <GL/glu.h>
#include <iostream>

int main() {
    // OpenGL initialization and rendering code

    // Example: Check OpenGL errors using gldebug
    GLenum error = glGetError();
    if (error != GL_NO_ERROR) {
        std::cerr << "OpenGL Error: " << gluErrorString(error) <<
        std::endl;
    }

    return 0;
}
```

This fragment demonstrates the inclusion of OpenGL headers, basic initialization, and an example of checking for OpenGL errors using gldebug.

Overview of game engines and frameworks

leveraging game engines and frameworks is a common practice. These tools provide a structured environment, pre-built modules, and essential functionalities, allowing developers to focus on creating engaging gameplay rather than reinventing the wheel.

Understanding Game Engines

Definition and Purpose

A game engine is a software framework designed to simplify and expedite the development of video games. It serves as the backbone of a game, handling various aspects such as rendering, physics, audio, input, and more. Game engines aim to provide developers with a set of tools and abstractions to streamline the creation of interactive and immersive experiences.

Features of Game Engines

- **Graphics Rendering:** Game engines excel in rendering graphics efficiently, managing everything from 2D sprites to complex 3D models. They often incorporate rendering pipelines, shaders, and optimizations to deliver visually stunning environments.
- **Physics Simulation:** Many game engines include physics engines to simulate realistic interactions between game objects. This involves handling collisions, gravity, and other physical phenomena to enhance gameplay realism.
- **Audio Processing:** Sound plays a crucial role in gaming immersion. Game engines come equipped with audio systems that handle playback, spatial positioning, and effects to create a captivating auditory experience.
- **Input Handling:** Managing user input is a fundamental aspect of game development. Game engines simplify this process by providing abstractions for handling keyboard, mouse, controller, and touch inputs.
- **Scene Management:** Games often consist of multiple scenes or levels. Game engines facilitate the creation, loading, and management of these scenes, allowing for seamless transitions and efficient memory usage.
- **Scripting Support:** To enhance flexibility, game engines often support scripting languages. This allows developers to implement game logic and behavior without recompiling the entire codebase.

Example: Utilizing Unreal Engine

Unreal Engine, a popular game engine, is known for its versatility and robust feature set. Below is a simple example of a C++ class within Unreal Engine:

```cpp
#include "GameFramework/Actor.h"
#include "MyGameActor.generated.h"

UCLASS()
class MYGAME_API AMyGameActor : public AActor {
```

```
    GENERATED_BODY()

public:
    // Sets default values for this actor's properties
    AMyGameActor();

    // Called every frame
    virtual void Tick(float DeltaTime) override;

protected:
    // Called when the game starts or when spawned
    virtual void BeginPlay() override;
};
```

This snippet showcases the definition of a basic game actor class in Unreal Engine, demonstrating the framework's syntax and structure.

Exploring Game Frameworks

Definition and Purpose

While game engines provide a comprehensive environment for game development, frameworks offer a more modular and customizable approach. Game frameworks are sets of libraries and tools that focus on specific aspects of game development, allowing developers to mix and match components based on their project's requirements.

Features of Game Frameworks

- **Modularity:** Game frameworks are often modular, allowing developers to select and integrate only the components needed for their specific game. This promotes a more lightweight and tailored development experience.
- **Flexibility:** Unlike all-encompassing game engines, frameworks provide greater flexibility. Developers have more control over the architecture of their game and can choose specific components based on their preferences.

- **Learning Curve:** Game frameworks, being more lightweight, often have a gentler learning curve compared to full-fledged game engines. This can be advantageous for smaller teams or solo developers.
- **Targeted Functionality:** Frameworks may specialize in certain aspects of game development, such as physics, AI, or networking. This allows developers to integrate specific functionalities without unnecessary overhead.

Example: Utilizing SFML (Simple and Fast Multimedia Library)

SFML is a multimedia library that provides components for 2D game development. Below is a simplified example of using SFML to create a window and display a sprite:

```cpp
#include <SFML/Graphics.hpp>

int main() {
    // Create a window
    sf::RenderWindow window(sf::VideoMode(800, 600), "SFML Game");

    // Load a texture and create a sprite
    sf::Texture texture;
    texture.loadFromFile("sprite.png");
    sf::Sprite sprite(texture);

    // Main game loop
    while (window.isOpen()) {
        // Handle events
        sf::Event event;
        while (window.pollEvent(event)) {
            if (event.type == sf::Event::Closed)
                window.close();
        }

        // Clear the window
        window.clear();

        // Draw the sprite
```

```
        window.draw(sprite);

        // Display the contents
        window.display();
    }

    return 0;
}
```

This example illustrates the simplicity of creating a window and displaying a sprite using SFML, showcasing the streamlined approach of a game framework.

Setting up development environments

Setting up a robust development environment is the first step towards embarking on a successful C++ game development journey. This section will guide you through the process of establishing a conducive workspace, choosing the right tools, and configuring your development environment for seamless coding. Let's delve into the essential components of setting up your C++ development environment.

Choosing a C++ Compiler

The compiler is a crucial tool that translates your human-readable C++ code into machine-readable instructions. There are various C++ compilers available, and your choice might depend on factors like platform compatibility, performance, and personal preference.

Example: Using GCC (GNU Compiler Collection)

GCC is a widely used open-source compiler known for its portability and efficiency. Below is a simple "Hello, World!" program compiled using GCC:

```cpp
#include <iostream>

int main() {
    std::cout << "Hello, World!" << std::endl;
    return 0;
}
```

Compile the code using the following command in the terminal:

```
g++ hello_world.cpp -o hello_world
```

This generates an executable named **hello_world** that you can run to see the output.

Integrated Development Environments (IDEs)

IDEs provide a comprehensive environment for software development, offering features like code editing, debugging, and project management. Choosing the right IDE can significantly enhance your productivity.

Example: Visual Studio Code

Visual Studio Code is a lightweight yet powerful IDE with excellent support for C++ development. After installing the "C/C++" extension, you can create a new project and write code. Here's a snippet:

```cpp
#include <iostream>

int main() {
    std::cout << "Hello, Visual Studio Code!" << std::endl;
    return 0;
}
```

Visual Studio Code simplifies the development process by providing features like IntelliSense for code completion and integrated debugging capabilities.

Setting up a Project Structure

Organizing your project structure is essential for maintaining a clean and understandable codebase. Create a structured layout with directories for source code, headers, assets, and build files.

Example Project Structure:

```
MyGameProject/
|-- src/
|    |-- main.cpp
|-- include/
|    |-- game.h
|-- assets/
|-- build/
|-- CMakeLists.txt
```

Build Systems

A build system automates the process of compiling your code, linking dependencies, and creating the final executable. CMake is a popular cross-platform build system that simplifies this process.

Example: CMakeLists.txt

Create a **CMakeLists.txt** file in the root of your project:

```
cmake_minimum_required(VERSION 3.10)
project(MyGameProject)
set(CMAKE_CXX_STANDARD 14)
add_executable(MyGameProject src/main.cpp)
```

This CMakeLists.txt file specifies the minimum required CMake version, sets the C++ standard, and declares the executable and its source file.

Version Control

Using version control is essential for tracking changes, collaborating with others, and managing your project's history. Git is a widely used version control system.

Example: Basic Git Commands

Initialize a Git repository:

```
git init
```

Add your files to the repository:

```
git add .
```

Commit the changes:

```
git commit -m "Initial commit"
```

Utilizing development tools for C++ game programming

In the world of C++ game development, proficiency with development tools is essential for efficiency, collaboration, and the creation of high-quality games. This part explores a variety of development tools that can enhance your C++ game programming experience, from debugging and profiling to code editors and collaboration platforms.

Code Editors and Integrated Development Environments (IDEs)

Visual Studio

Visual Studio is a robust IDE that provides a comprehensive environment for C++ game development. It offers features like IntelliSense for code completion, integrated debugging, and project management tools. Below is an example of a simple C++ program within Visual Studio:

```cpp
#include <iostream>

int main() {
    std::cout << "Hello, Visual Studio!" << std::endl;
    return 0;
}
```

Visual Studio streamlines the development process, offering a user-friendly interface and powerful capabilities.

Visual Studio Code

Visual Studio Code, a lightweight and versatile code editor, is well-suited for C++ game development. With the addition of relevant extensions, it provides IntelliSense, debugging support, and Git integration. Here's a basic example in Visual Studio Code:

```cpp
#include <iostream>

int main() {
    std::cout << "Hello, Visual Studio Code!" << std::endl;
    return 0;
}
```

Visual Studio Code's extensibility makes it adaptable to different workflows and preferences.

Debugging Tools

GDB (GNU Debugger)

GDB is a powerful debugger that aids in identifying and fixing issues in C++ code. It allows developers to set breakpoints, inspect variables, and step through the code. Consider the following example:

```cpp
#include <iostream>

int main() {
    int x = 5;
    int y = 10;

    // Set a breakpoint here to inspect variables
    int result = x + y;

    std::cout << "Result: " << result << std::endl;

    return 0;
}
```

Using GDB, developers can step through the code and examine the values of **x**, **y**, and **result** to identify potential issues.

Profiling Tools

Valgrind

Valgrind is a tool for detecting memory leaks and profiling C++ code. Let's consider a scenario where Valgrind is used to check for memory leaks:

```cpp
#include <iostream>
#include <cstdlib>

int main() {
    // Allocate memory without freeing it
    int* dynamicArray = new int[100];

    // Accessing memory to avoid compiler optimizations
    std::cout << dynamicArray[0] << std::endl;
```

```
    // Missing delete[] to free the allocated memory

    return 0;
}
```

Running this program through Valgrind would identify the memory leak and provide insights into memory usage.

Build Systems

CMake

CMake simplifies the build process, enabling developers to generate platform-specific build files. Its cross-platform nature makes it an excellent choice for C++ game development. Consider the following example:

```
cmake_minimum_required(VERSION 3.10)

project(MyGameProject)

set(CMAKE_CXX_STANDARD 14)

add_executable(MyGameProject main.cpp)
```

This CMakeLists.txt file sets up a basic C++ project, specifying the minimum CMake version, the project name, and the source file.

Collaboration Tools

Git and GitHub

Git is a distributed version control system, and GitHub is a web-based platform that facilitates collaborative software development. Using these tools enables version control, collaboration, and code sharing. Here's a simple example of using Git:

```
git init
git add .
git commit -m "Initial commit"
```

Uploading the repository to GitHub further enhances collaboration, allowing multiple developers to work on the same project.

Graphics and Visualization Tools

OpenGL Debugger (gldebug)

For game developers working with OpenGL, tools like gldebug provide insights into the graphics rendering process. The following example illustrates a basic usage scenario:

```
#include <GL/gl.h>
#include <GL/glu.h>
#include <iostream>

int main() {
    // Initialize OpenGL and rendering code

    // Example: Check OpenGL errors using gldebug
    GLenum error = glGetError();
    if (error != GL_NO_ERROR) {
        std::cerr << "OpenGL Error: " << gluErrorString(error) <<
        std::endl;
    }

    return 0;
}
```

This snippet demonstrates the inclusion of OpenGL headers, basic initialization, and an example of checking for OpenGL errors using gldebug.

Audio Tools

FMOD Studio

FMOD Studio is an audio middleware solution that simplifies the integration of dynamic and immersive audio into games. While FMOD Studio often involves integrating with the game engine, below is a simplified example of playing a sound using FMOD:

```cpp
#include <fmod.hpp>
#include <iostream>

int main() {
    // Initialize FMOD and load a sound

    // Example: Play the loaded sound
    std::cout << "Playing sound..." << std::endl;

    // Cleanup FMOD resources

    return 0;
}
```

This example highlights the essential steps involved in integrating audio using FMOD.

Networking Tools

RakNet

RakNet is a C++ networking engine for building multiplayer games. Although RakNet is no longer being actively developed, it provides a historical example of networking in C++. A simplified example involves initializing RakNet, creating a server, and handling network messages.

```cpp
#include <RakPeerInterface.h>
#include <MessageIdentifiers.h>
#include <BitStream.h>
#include <iostream>

int main() {
    // Initialize RakNet

    // Create a server

    // Handle network messages

    // Cleanup RakNet resources

    return 0;
}
```

This snippet showcases the basic structure of a networking program using RakNet.

Integrated AI Tools

OpenAI GPT (Generative Pre-trained Transformer)

OpenAI GPT, while not a traditional game AI tool, can be utilized to create dynamic and responsive in-game dialogues or behaviors. An example might involve integrating GPT to generate dialogues based on player interactions.

```cpp
#include <iostream>
#include <string>

// Function to generate AI-driven dialogue
std::string generateAIResponse(const std::string& playerInput) {
    // Connect to OpenAI GPT API and send playerInput
    // Receive AI-generated response
```

```cpp
    std::string aiResponse = "AI: " + playerInput + " ...
    AI-generated response.";

    return aiResponse;
}

int main() {
    // Game loop
    while (true) {
        // Get player input
        std::string playerInput;
        std::cout << "Player: ";
        std::getline(std::cin, playerInput);

        // Generate AI response
        std::string aiResponse = generateAIResponse(playerInput);

        // Display AI response
        std::cout << aiResponse << std::endl;
    }

    return 0;
}
```

This section covered an overview of game engines and frameworks, as well as how to use development tools for C++ game programming and set up development environments. As you proceed with your C++ game development journey, every tool—from code editors and integrated development environments to debugging, profiling, and communication tools—becomes increasingly important in helping to streamline the process.

Design Patterns for Game Development

Design patterns and implementation in game development

Design patterns are essential tools for structuring and organizing code in a way that promotes flexibility, maintainability, and scalability. In this chapter, we'll explore several design patterns commonly used in C++ game development. Each pattern addresses specific challenges encountered in game programming, providing elegant solutions to common problems.

Singleton Pattern

The Singleton pattern ensures that a class has only one instance and provides a global point of access to that instance. This is particularly useful for managing global game state or resources.

Example:

```cpp
class GameManager {
private:
    static GameManager* instance;

    // Private constructor to prevent instantiation
```

```cpp
    GameManager() {}

public:
    // Method to access the singleton instance
    static GameManager* getInstance() {
        if (!instance) {
            instance = new GameManager();
        }
        return instance;
    }

    // Other methods and properties...
};

// Initialization of the static member
GameManager* GameManager::instance = nullptr;
```

Usage:

```cpp
// Accessing the singleton instance
GameManager* gameManager = GameManager::getInstance();
```

Factory Pattern

The Factory pattern provides an interface for creating families of related or dependent objects without specifying their concrete classes. It's useful for creating game objects based on certain conditions.

Example:

```cpp
class GameObject {
public:
    virtual void draw() = 0;
    virtual ~GameObject() {}
};
```

```cpp
class Enemy : public GameObject {
public:
    void draw() override {
        // Drawing logic for an enemy
    }
};


class PowerUp : public GameObject {
public:
    void draw() override {
        // Drawing logic for a power-up
    }
};


class GameObjectFactory {
public:
    virtual GameObject* createGameObject() = 0;
    virtual ~GameObjectFactory() {}
};


class EnemyFactory : public GameObjectFactory {
public:
    GameObject* createGameObject() override {
        return new Enemy();
    }
};


class PowerUpFactory : public GameObjectFactory {
public:
    GameObject* createGameObject() override {
        return new PowerUp();
    }
};
```

Usage:

```cpp
// Using a factory to create game objects
GameObjectFactory* factory = new EnemyFactory();
```

```
GameObject* enemy = factory->createGameObject();
```

Observer Pattern

The Observer pattern defines a one-to-many dependency between objects, so that when one object changes state, all its dependents are notified and updated automatically. This is useful for implementing event systems in games.

Example:

```cpp
#include <iostream>
#include <vector>

class Observer {
public:
    virtual void update() = 0;
    virtual ~Observer() {}
};

class Subject {
private:
    std::vector<Observer*> observers;

public:
    void addObserver(Observer* observer) {
        observers.push_back(observer);
    }

    void removeObserver(Observer* observer) {
        // Remove observer logic
    }

    void notifyObservers() {
        for (Observer* observer : observers) {
            observer->update();
        }
```

```cpp
    }
};

class Player : public Observer {
public:
    void update() override {
        std::cout << "Player has been updated!" << std::endl;
    }
};

class ScoreManager : public Observer {
public:
    void update() override {
        std::cout << "Score has been updated!" << std::endl;
    }
};
```

Usage:

```cpp
// Creating subjects and observers
Subject gameSubject;
Player playerObserver;
ScoreManager scoreObserver;

// Adding observers to the subject
gameSubject.addObserver(&playerObserver);
gameSubject.addObserver(&scoreObserver);

// Notifying observers
gameSubject.notifyObservers();
```

State Pattern

The State pattern allows an object to alter its behavior when its internal state changes. This pattern is beneficial when an object has multiple states and transitions between them.

Example:

```cpp
#include <iostream>

class GameState;

class GameContext {
private:
    GameState* currentState;

public:
    GameContext();

    void setState(GameState* state);
    void request();

    // Other methods...
};

class GameState {
public:
    virtual void handleInput(GameContext* context) = 0;
    virtual ~GameState() {}
};

class MenuState : public GameState {
public:
    void handleInput(GameContext* context) override {
        std::cout << "Menu state handling input." << std::endl;
    }
};

class PlayingState : public GameState {
public:
    void handleInput(GameContext* context) override {
        std::cout << "Playing state handling input." << std::endl;
    }
};

// Implementation of GameContext and other classes...
```

Usage:

```cpp
// Creating a game context
GameContext game;

// Setting the initial state
game.setState(new MenuState());

// Requesting actions based on the state
game.request();   // Outputs: Menu state handling input.

// Changing the state
game.setState(new PlayingState());
game.request();   // Outputs: Playing state handling input.
```

Command Pattern

The Command pattern encapsulates a request as an object, thereby allowing for parameterization of clients with different requests, queuing of requests, and logging of the parameters. This is useful for implementing input systems and undo/redo functionalities in games.

Example:

```cpp
#include <iostream>

class Command {
public:
    virtual void execute() = 0;
    virtual ~Command() {}
};

class JumpCommand : public Command {
public:
    void execute() override {
```

```cpp
        std::cout << "Player jumping!" << std::endl;
    }
};

class ShootCommand : public Command {
public:
    void execute() override {
        std::cout << "Player shooting!" << std::endl;
    }
};

class InputHandler {
private:
    Command* buttonA;
    Command* buttonB;

public:
    InputHandler(Command* a, Command* b) : buttonA(a), buttonB(b)
    {}

    void handleInputA() {
        buttonA->execute();
    }

    void handleInputB() {
        buttonB->execute();
    }
};
```

Usage:

```cpp
// Creating commands
JumpCommand jump;
ShootCommand shoot;

// Creating an input handler with commands
InputHandler inputHandler(&jump, &shoot);
```

```
// Handling inputs
inputHandler.handleInputA();  // Outputs: Player jumping!
inputHandler.handleInputB();  // Outputs: Player shooting!
```

Design patterns provide solutions to recurring problems, promoting code reusability, maintainability, and scalability. Incorporating these patterns into your game development projects can lead to more robust and flexible code, making your games easier to develop and maintain over time.

Best practices and considerations for scalable game architecture

Creating a scalable and maintainable game architecture is crucial for the success of any C++ game development project. Let's explore explore best practices and considerations to ensure your game architecture can adapt and scale as your project grows. The examples provided will illustrate how these practices can be implemented in C++.

Modularization and Component-Based Architecture

Best Practice:

Organize your game code into modular components to promote reusability and maintainability. Implement a component-based architecture where game entities are composed of independent, reusable components.

Implementation:

```cpp
class TransformComponent {
public:
    float x, y, z;
    // Other transformation-related properties and methods...
};
```

```cpp
class RenderComponent {
public:
    void render() {
        // Rendering logic...
    }
    // Other rendering-related properties and methods...
};


class GameObject {
private:
    TransformComponent transform;
    RenderComponent render;

public:
    void update() {
        transform.update();
        render.render();
    }
};
```

Utilize Smart Pointers for Resource Management

Best Practice:

Use smart pointers (such as **std::shared_ptr** or **std::unique_ptr**) for managing memory and resources to minimize the risk of memory leaks and simplify resource cleanup.

Implementation:

```cpp
#include <memory>

class Texture {
    // Texture implementation...
};
```

```cpp
class Sprite {
private:
    std::shared_ptr<Texture> texture;

public:
    Sprite(std::shared_ptr<Texture> tex) : texture(tex) {}

    // Sprite methods...
};
```

Event Systems for Decoupled Communication

Best Practice:

Implement an event system to facilitate communication between different parts of the game without creating direct dependencies. This promotes loose coupling, making your code more flexible.

Implementation:

```cpp
#include <functional>
#include <vector>

class EventManager {
private:
    std::vector<std::function<void()>> subscribers;

public:
    void subscribe(const std::function<void()>& callback) {
        subscribers.push_back(callback);
    }

    void publish() {
        for (const auto& subscriber : subscribers) {
```

```cpp
            subscriber();
        }
    }
};

// Example Usage:

class Player {
public:
    void onPlayerDeath() {
        // Handle player death...
    }
};

int main() {
    EventManager eventManager;

    Player player;

    // Subscribe the player's death handler
    eventManager.subscribe(std::bind(&Player::onPlayerDeath,
    &player));

    // Publish the event when the player dies
    eventManager.publish();

    return 0;
}
```

Efficient Memory Management

Best Practice:

Optimize memory usage by considering the memory layout of data structures, minimizing cache misses, and avoiding unnecessary allocations. Implement object pools for frequently created and destroyed objects.

Implementation:

```cpp
#include <vector>

class Bullet {
    // Bullet implementation...
};

class BulletPool {
private:
    std::vector<Bullet> pool;
    std::vector<Bullet*> activeBullets;

public:
    Bullet* createBullet() {
        if (pool.empty()) {
            pool.emplace_back();
        }

        Bullet* newBullet = &pool.back();
        pool.pop_back();
        activeBullets.push_back(newBullet);

        return newBullet;
    }

    void destroyBullet(Bullet* bullet) {
        // Reset bullet state...
        activeBullets.erase(std::remove(activeBullets.begin(),
        activeBullets.end(), bullet), activeBullets.end());
        pool.push_back(*bullet);
    }
};
```

Optimize for Cache Coherency

Best Practice:

Design your data structures and algorithms to maximize cache coherency, reducing the impact of cache misses and improving performance.

Implementation:

```cpp
struct GameObject {
    float x, y, z;
    // Other properties...

    // Methods...
};

class GameObjectManager {
private:
    std::vector<GameObject> gameObjects;

public:
    void updateAll() {
        for (auto& gameObject : gameObjects) {
            gameObject.update();
        }
    }
};
```

Use Compile-Time Polymorphism Where Possible

Best Practice:

Prefer compile-time polymorphism (templates) over runtime polymorphism (virtual functions) when applicable to maximize performance.

Implementation:

```cpp
template <typename T>
class Component {
public:
    void update() {
        static_cast<T*>(this)->updateImpl();
    }
};

class TransformComponent : public Component<TransformComponent> {
public:
    void updateImpl() {
        // Update transformation logic...
    }
};

class RenderComponent : public Component<RenderComponent> {
public:
    void updateImpl() {
        // Update rendering logic...
    }
};
```

Design concepts and best practices must be carefully considered when implementing scalable game architecture in C++. You can create a solid basis for your game by employing compile-time polymorphism, optimizing for cache coherency, implementing efficient memory management, modularizing your code, and utilizing smart pointers.

These techniques enhance scalability while simultaneously enhancing performance and maintainability of the code. Don't forget to modify these guidelines to fit the particular needs of your gaming project.

Graphics and Rendering

Graphics Rendering with C++

One essential component of game creation that directly affects players' visual experience is graphics rendering. We'll go over important ideas and methods for putting graphics rendering in C++ into practice in this chapter. We'll go over shaders and rendering pipelines and give real-world examples to show how graphics rendering is implemented in games.

Introduction to Graphics Rendering

The process of turning 3D scenes and models into 2D pictures that are shown on a screen is known as graphics rendering. A pipeline that includes steps like geometry processing, rasterization, and pixel shading is commonly used in the rendering process.

Setting up a Simple Rendering Framework

Implementation:

```cpp
#include <iostream>

class GraphicsRenderer {
public:
    void initialize() {
        // Initialize graphics renderer...
        std::cout << "Graphics renderer initialized." << std::endl;
    }
```

```cpp
    void renderFrame() {
        // Render a frame...
        std::cout << "Rendering a frame." << std::endl;
    }

    void cleanup() {
        // Cleanup resources...
        std::cout << "Graphics renderer cleaned up." << std::endl;
    }
};

int main() {
    // Initialize graphics renderer
    GraphicsRenderer renderer;
    renderer.initialize();

    // Render frames (in the game loop)
    for (int frame = 0; frame < 60; ++frame) {
        renderer.renderFrame();
    }

    // Cleanup
    renderer.cleanup();

    return 0;
}
```

Shader Programming

Shaders are small programs that run on the GPU and are crucial for rendering realistic graphics. They define how light interacts with surfaces and how colors are determined.

Implementation (Vertex Shader):

```
#version 330 core

layout (location = 0) in vec3 position;

void main() {
    gl_Position = vec4(position, 1.0);
}
```

Implementation (Fragment Shader):

```
#version 330 core

out vec4 FragColor;

void main() {
    FragColor = vec4(1.0, 0.0, 0.0, 1.0); // Red color
}
```

OpenGL for Graphics Rendering

OpenGL is a widely used graphics API that provides a cross-platform framework for rendering 2D and 3D graphics.

Implementation (OpenGL Setup):

```
#include <GL/glew.h>
#include <GLFW/glfw3.h>

int main() {
    // Initialize GLFW
    if (!glfwInit()) {
        return -1;
    }

    // Create a windowed mode window and its OpenGL context
```

```cpp
    GLFWwindow* window = glfwCreateWindow(640, 480, "OpenGL
    Window", NULL, NULL);
    if (!window) {
        glfwTerminate();
        return -1;
    }

    // Make the window's context current
    glfwMakeContextCurrent(window);

    // Initialize GLEW
    if (glewInit() != GLEW_OK) {
        return -1;
    }

    // Main loop
    while (!glfwWindowShouldClose(window)) {
        // Render here
        glClear(GL_COLOR_BUFFER_BIT);

        // Swap front and back buffers
        glfwSwapBuffers(window);

        // Poll for and process events
        glfwPollEvents();
    }

    // Cleanup
    glfwTerminate();
    return 0;
}
```

Rendering a Simple Triangle

Implementation (OpenGL Triangle Rendering):

```cpp
#include <GL/glew.h>
#include <GLFW/glfw3.h>

int main() {
    // Initialize GLFW
    if (!glfwInit()) {
        return -1;
    }

    // Create a windowed mode window and its OpenGL context
    GLFWwindow* window = glfwCreateWindow(640, 480, "OpenGL
    Triangle", NULL, NULL);
    if (!window) {
        glfwTerminate();
        return -1;
    }

    // Make the window's context current
    glfwMakeContextCurrent(window);

    // Initialize GLEW
    if (glewInit() != GLEW_OK) {
        return -1;
    }

    // Define the vertices of a triangle
    float vertices[] = {
        -0.5f, -0.5f, 0.0f,
         0.5f, -0.5f, 0.0f,
         0.0f,  0.5f, 0.0f
    };

    // Create a vertex array object (VAO) and vertex buffer object
    (VBO)
    GLuint VAO, VBO;
    glGenVertexArrays(1, &VAO);
    glGenBuffers(1, &VBO);

    // Bind the VAO
    glBindVertexArray(VAO);
```

```cpp
    // Bind and initialize the VBO
    glBindBuffer(GL_ARRAY_BUFFER, VBO);
    glBufferData(GL_ARRAY_BUFFER, sizeof(vertices), vertices,
    GL_STATIC_DRAW);

    // Specify the vertex attribute pointers
    glVertexAttribPointer(0, 3, GL_FLOAT, GL_FALSE, 3 *
    sizeof(float), (void*)0);
    glEnableVertexAttribArray(0);

    // Unbind the VAO and VBO
    glBindBuffer(GL_ARRAY_BUFFER, 0);
    glBindVertexArray(0);

    // Main loop
    while (!glfwWindowShouldClose(window)) {
        // Render here
        glClear(GL_COLOR_BUFFER_BIT);

        // Use the shader program (not shown for brevity)

        // Bind the VAO
        glBindVertexArray(VAO);

        // Draw the triangle
        glDrawArrays(GL_TRIANGLES, 0, 3);

        // Unbind the VAO
        glBindVertexArray(0);

        // Swap front and back buffers
        glfwSwapBuffers(window);

        // Poll for and process events
        glfwPollEvents();
    }

    // Cleanup
    glDeleteVertexArrays(1, &VAO);
```

```
    glDeleteBuffers(1, &VBO);

    glfwTerminate();
    return 0;
}
```

A challenging yet essential component of game creation is graphics rendering. We went over the fundamentals of configuring a rendering framework, gave an overview of shader programming, looked at the OpenGL graphics API, and rendered a basic triangle. Understanding and mastering graphics rendering will help you create visually stunning and immersive gaming experiences as you advance in your C++ game development career.

Utilizing DirectX for rendering

Microsoft created DirectX, a potent collection of APIs that offers extensive support for graphics, audio, and input in Windows-based game creation. Let's examine the fundamentals of configuring DirectX for C++ rendering and offer real-world examples to highlight important ideas.

Setting up a Basic DirectX Application

Implementation:

```cpp
#include <Windows.h>
#include <d3d11.h>

LRESULT CALLBACK WindowProc(HWND hwnd, UINT uMsg, WPARAM wParam,
LPARAM lParam) {
    switch (uMsg) {
        case WM_DESTROY:
            PostQuitMessage(0);
            return 0;
        default:
```

```cpp
        return DefWindowProc(hwnd, uMsg, wParam, lParam);
    }
}

int main() {
    // Register the window class
    WNDCLASS wc = {};
    wc.lpfnWndProc = WindowProc;
    wc.hInstance = GetModuleHandle(NULL);
    wc.lpszClassName = L"DirectXWindowClass";
    RegisterClass(&wc);

    // Create the window
    HWND hwnd = CreateWindowEx(0, L"DirectXWindowClass", L"DirectX
    Window", WS_OVERLAPPEDWINDOW, CW_USEDEFAULT, CW_USEDEFAULT,
    800, 600, 0, 0, GetModuleHandle(NULL), 0);

    // Initialize DirectX
    D3D_FEATURE_LEVEL featureLevels[] = { D3D_FEATURE_LEVEL_11_0,
    D3D_FEATURE_LEVEL_10_1 };
    ID3D11Device* device;
    ID3D11DeviceContext* deviceContext;
    D3D11CreateDevice(NULL, D3D_DRIVER_TYPE_HARDWARE, NULL, 0,
    featureLevels, 2, D3D11_SDK_VERSION, &device, NULL,
    &deviceContext);

    // Main loop
    MSG msg = {};
    while (msg.message != WM_QUIT) {
        if (PeekMessage(&msg, 0, 0, 0, PM_REMOVE)) {
            TranslateMessage(&msg);
            DispatchMessage(&msg);
        } else {
            // Rendering code goes here...

            // Swap buffers
            // ...

            // Poll for and process events
            // ...
```

```
        }
    }

    // Cleanup
    device->Release();
    deviceContext->Release();

    return 0;
}
```

Creating a Simple DirectX Vertex Shader and Pixel Shader

Implementation:

```
// Vertex Shader
struct VS_INPUT {
    float3 position : POSITION;
};

struct VS_OUTPUT {
    float4 position : SV_POSITION;
};

VS_OUTPUT main(VS_INPUT input) {
    VS_OUTPUT output;
    output.position = float4(input.position, 1.0f);
    return output;
}


// Pixel Shader
float4 main(VS_OUTPUT input) : SV_TARGET {
    return float4(1.0f, 0.0f, 0.0f, 1.0f); // Red color
}
```

Compiling and Loading Shaders in DirectX

Implementation:

```cpp
#include <d3dcompiler.h>

// Function to compile shaders
HRESULT CompileShader(LPCWSTR filePath, LPCSTR entryPoint, LPCSTR
shaderModel, ID3DBlob** blob) {
    HRESULT hr = S_OK;

    DWORD shaderFlags = D3DCOMPILE_ENABLE_STRICTNESS;
    #if defined( DEBUG ) || defined( _DEBUG )
        shaderFlags |= D3DCOMPILE_DEBUG;
    #endif

    ID3DBlob* errorBlob = nullptr;
    hr = D3DCompileFromFile(filePath, nullptr,
    D3D_COMPILE_STANDARD_FILE_INCLUDE, entryPoint, shaderModel,
    shaderFlags, 0, blob, &errorBlob);

    if (FAILED(hr)) {
        if (errorBlob) {
            OutputDebugStringA((char*)errorBlob->GetBufferPointer());
            errorBlob->Release();
        }
        return hr;
    }

    if (errorBlob) {
        errorBlob->Release();
    }

    return S_OK;
}

int main() {
    // ... (Initialization code)

    // Compile and load the vertex shader
    ID3DBlob* vsBlob = nullptr;
    HRESULT hr = CompileShader(L"VertexShader.hlsl", "main",
    "vs_5_0", &vsBlob);
    if (FAILED(hr)) {
```

```cpp
    // Handle shader compilation error
    return -1;
}

// Create the vertex shader
ID3D11VertexShader* vertexShader;
hr = device->CreateVertexShader(vsBlob->GetBufferPointer(),
vsBlob->GetBufferSize(), nullptr, &vertexShader);
if (FAILED(hr)) {
    // Handle shader creation error
    return -1;
}

// Compile and load the pixel shader
ID3DBlob* psBlob = nullptr;
hr = CompileShader(L"PixelShader.hlsl", "main", "ps_5_0",
&psBlob);
if (FAILED(hr)) {
    // Handle shader compilation error
    return -1;
}

// Create the pixel shader
ID3D11PixelShader* pixelShader;
hr = device->CreatePixelShader(psBlob->GetBufferPointer(),
psBlob->GetBufferSize(), nullptr, &pixelShader);
if (FAILED(hr)) {
    // Handle shader creation error
    return -1;
}

// Cleanup shader blobs
vsBlob->Release();
psBlob->Release();

// ... (Rendering code)

// Cleanup shaders
vertexShader->Release();
pixelShader->Release();
```

```
    // ... (Cleanup code)

    return 0;
 }
```

We've explored the fundamentals of utilizing DirectX for rendering in C++ game programming. We covered the setup of a basic DirectX application, the creation of a simple vertex and pixel shader, and the compilation and loading of shaders in DirectX. As you continue your journey in C++ game development, mastering DirectX will empower you to create visually compelling and immersive gaming experiences on the Windows platform.

GPU programming in C++

A key component of contemporary game creation is GPU programming, which enables creators to use the graphics processing units' (GPUs) parallel processing capacity for applications other than rendering, like intricate calculations and physics simulations. This part will discuss GPU programming with real-world examples from the C++ game development community.

Introduction to GPU Programming

Writing code for the GPU, which is very good at parallel processing, is known as GPU programming. C++ programmers can increase overall performance by using APIs like OpenCL and CUDA (Compute Unified Device Architecture) to offload particular workloads to the GPU.

Setting Up CUDA for GPU Programming in C++

Implementation:

```cpp
#include <iostream>
#include <cuda_runtime.h>

__global__ void gpuKernel(int* array, int size) {
    int tid = blockIdx.x * blockDim.x + threadIdx.x;
    if (tid < size) {
        array[tid] *= 2;
    }
}

int main() {
    const int arraySize = 10;
    int hostArray[arraySize] = {1, 2, 3, 4, 5, 6, 7, 8, 9, 10};

    int* deviceArray;
    cudaMalloc((void**)&deviceArray, arraySize * sizeof(int));
    cudaMemcpy(deviceArray, hostArray, arraySize * sizeof(int),
    cudaMemcpyHostToDevice);

    // Define block and grid dimensions
    dim3 blockSize(256);
    dim3 gridSize((arraySize + blockSize.x - 1) / blockSize.x);

    // Launch the kernel on the GPU
    gpuKernel<<<gridSize, blockSize>>>(deviceArray, arraySize);

    // Copy the results back to the host
    cudaMemcpy(hostArray, deviceArray, arraySize * sizeof(int),
    cudaMemcpyDeviceToHost);

    // Output the modified array
    std::cout << "Modified Array: ";
    for (int i = 0; i < arraySize; ++i) {
        std::cout << hostArray[i] << " ";
    }
    std::cout << std::endl;

    // Cleanup
    cudaFree(deviceArray);
```

```
    return 0;
}
```

GPU Programming with OpenCL in C++

Implementation:

```cpp
#include <iostream>
#include <CL/cl.hpp>

int main() {
    const int arraySize = 10;
    int hostArray[arraySize] = {1, 2, 3, 4, 5, 6, 7, 8, 9, 10};

    // Get available platforms
    std::vector<cl::Platform> platforms;
    cl::Platform::get(&platforms);

    // Select the first platform
    cl_context_properties properties[] = { CL_CONTEXT_PLATFORM,
    (cl_context_properties)(platforms[0])(), 0 };
    cl::Context context(CL_DEVICE_TYPE_GPU, properties);

    // Get available devices
    std::vector<cl::Device> devices =
    context.getInfo<CL_CONTEXT_DEVICES>();

    // Create a command queue
    cl::CommandQueue queue(context, devices[0]);

    // Create buffers for input and output
    cl::Buffer bufferInput(context, CL_MEM_READ_ONLY |
    CL_MEM_COPY_HOST_PTR, sizeof(int) * arraySize, hostArray);
    cl::Buffer bufferOutput(context, CL_MEM_WRITE_ONLY,
    sizeof(int) * arraySize);

    // Load and compile the OpenCL program
    cl::Program::Sources sources;
```

```cpp
    sources.push_back({ "kernel void gpuKernel(global int* array,
    const int size) { \
                        int gid = get_global_id(0); \
                        if (gid < size) { \
                          array[gid] *= 2; \
                        } \
                   }" });
    cl::Program program(context, sources);
    program.build(devices);

    // Create the kernel
    cl::Kernel kernel(program, "gpuKernel");
    kernel.setArg(0, bufferInput);
    kernel.setArg(1, arraySize);

    // Execute the kernel
    queue.enqueueNDRangeKernel(kernel, cl::NullRange,
    cl::NDRange(arraySize));

    // Read the results back to the host
    queue.enqueueReadBuffer(bufferInput, CL_TRUE, 0, sizeof(int) *
    arraySize, hostArray);

    // Output the modified array
    std::cout << "Modified Array: ";
    for (int i = 0; i < arraySize; ++i) {
        std::cout << hostArray[i] << " ";
    }
    std::cout << std::endl;

    return 0;
}
```

Integration with Graphics Rendering in C++ Game Development

GPU programming is often used in conjunction with graphics rendering for tasks such as physics simulations. Here's a simple example of integrating GPU programming with OpenGL.

Implementation:

```cpp
#include <iostream>
#include <GL/glew.h>
#include <GLFW/glfw3.h>
#include <cuda_runtime.h>

// CUDA kernel for updating vertex positions
__global__ void updateVertices(float* vertices, int size, float
deltaTime) {
    int tid = blockIdx.x * blockDim.x + threadIdx.x;
    if (tid < size) {
        vertices[tid * 3] += deltaTime; // Update X coordinate
    }
}

int main() {
    // ... (OpenGL initialization code)

    const int numVertices = 1000;
    float* vertices = new float[numVertices * 3];

    // ... (Initialize vertices)

    // CUDA setup
    float* deviceVertices;
    cudaMalloc((void**)&deviceVertices, numVertices * 3 *
    sizeof(float));
    cudaMemcpy(deviceVertices, vertices, numVertices * 3 *
    sizeof(float), cudaMemcpyHostToDevice);

    // ... (OpenGL vertex buffer setup)

    // Main loop
    while (!glfwWindowShouldClose(window)) {
        // ... (OpenGL rendering code)

        // CUDA kernel launch for updating vertices
        dim3 blockSize(256);
        dim3 gridSize((numVertices + blockSize.x - 1) /
```

```cpp
    blockSize.x);
    updateVertices<<<gridSize, blockSize>>>(deviceVertices,
    numVertices, deltaTime);

    // Copy updated vertices back to host
    cudaMemcpy(vertices, deviceVertices, numVertices * 3 *
    sizeof(float), cudaMemcpyDeviceToHost);

    // ... (Update OpenGL vertex buffer)

    // Poll for and process events
    glfwPollEvents();
  }

  // Cleanup
  delete[] vertices;
  cudaFree(deviceVertices);

  // ... (OpenGL cleanup code)

  return 0;
}
```

By enabling parallel processing, GPU programming in C++ game development allows developers to shift computationally demanding tasks to the GPU. In the framework of a C++ game development project, we studied GPU programming with CUDA and OpenCL and showed how it can be combined with graphics rendering. You'll find ways to improve and optimize different parts of your games as you learn more about GPU programming.

Optimizing Graphics Performance

A crucial component of game creation is graphics performance optimization, which guarantees gamers a fluid and responsive experience. This chapter will discuss and offer real-world examples of several methods for improving graphics speed in C++ game programming.

When developing C++ games, optimizing graphics performance is an ongoing process that calls for knowledge of the hardware, effective rendering methods, and the use of profiling tools. This section will cover tactics to increase graphics efficiency, such as batch rendering, texture atlases, shader optimization, Level of Detail (LOD) techniques, and asynchronous asset loading.

Profiling and Analysis Tools

It's crucial to use profiling and analytic tools to find performance bottlenecks before implementing optimization approaches. Applications like AMD Radeon GPU Profiler, NVIDIA Nsight, and Intel Graphics Performance Analyzers (GPA) can offer insightful data about how well an application performs.

Batch Rendering for Efficiency

In batch rendering, the overhead of state changes is minimized by concatenating several draw operations into one call. This optimization works especially well when rendering a lot of objects with identical characteristics.

Implementation:

```cpp
// Example of batch rendering using OpenGL
void renderBatch(const std::vector<RenderObject>& renderObjects) {
    // Set common rendering state (shaders, textures, etc.)

    for (const auto& object : renderObjects) {
        // Set object-specific state (transformation matrix,
        material properties, etc.)

        // Issue draw call
        glDrawElements(GL_TRIANGLES, object.indexCount,
        GL_UNSIGNED_INT, (void*)(object.startIndex *
        sizeof(GLuint)));
    }
}
```

Level of Detail (LOD) Techniques

Simplified models are used when distant from the camera in order to use Level of Detail approaches. As a result, performance is enhanced by rendering fewer polygons.

Implementation:

```cpp
// Example of LOD implementation using OpenGL
void renderObjectWithLOD(const RenderObject& object, float
distanceFromCamera) {
    if (distanceFromCamera < LOD_DISTANCE_HIGH) {
        // Render high-detail model
        // ...
    } else if (distanceFromCamera < LOD_DISTANCE_MEDIUM) {
        // Render medium-detail model
        // ...
    } else {
        // Render low-detail model
```

```
        // ...
    }
}
```

Texture Atlases for Efficient Texture Management

With texture atlases, you may reduce the amount of texture binds and increase rendering efficiency by consolidating many textures into a single texture.

Implementation:

```cpp
// Example of texture atlas usage using OpenGL
void renderWithTextureAtlas(const TextureAtlas& atlas, const
RenderObject& object) {
    // Bind the texture atlas
    glBindTexture(GL_TEXTURE_2D, atlas.textureID);

    // Set texture coordinates for the specific object
    // ...

    // Issue draw call
    glDrawElements(GL_TRIANGLES, object.indexCount,
    GL_UNSIGNED_INT, (void*)(object.startIndex * sizeof(GLuint)));
}
```

Shader Optimization

Optimizing shaders involves reducing unnecessary calculations and ensuring that they are efficient for the target hardware.

Implementation:

```cpp
// Example of shader optimization
float calculateLighting(vec3 normal, vec3 lightDirection) {
```

```
    // Normalize vectors outside the shader if possible
    normal = normalize(normal);
    lightDirection = normalize(lightDirection);

    // Perform lighting calculations
    float intensity = max(dot(normal, lightDirection), 0.0);
    return intensity;
}
```

Asynchronous Loading of Assets

Loading assets asynchronously ensures that the game doesn't freeze during loading times. Use separate threads or asynchronous techniques to load assets in the background.

Implementation:

```cpp
// Example of asynchronous asset loading using std::async
#include <future>

std::future<void> loadAssetsAsync() {
    return std::async(std::launch::async, [] {
        // Load assets in the background
        // ...
    });
}
```

As you apply these techniques and dig deeper into optimization, you'll be able to create games that provide a seamless and immersive experience for players.

Techniques for efficient rendering

Creating games that are both responsive and aesthetically spectacular requires efficient rendering. This section will cover several rendering strategies for C++ game programming, along with real-world examples to highlight important ideas.

Instanced Rendering for Batch Efficiency

By using a single draw call to render many instances of an object, instanced rendering lowers CPU overhead and boosts efficiency.

Implementation:

```cpp
// Example of instanced rendering using OpenGL
void renderInstanced(const RenderObject& object, const
std::vector<glm::mat4>& instanceTransforms) {
    // Set common rendering state (shaders, textures, etc.)

    // Set object-specific state (transformation matrix, material
    properties, etc.)

    // Bind VBO for instance transforms
    glBindBuffer(GL_ARRAY_BUFFER, instanceTransformsVBO);
    glBufferData(GL_ARRAY_BUFFER, instanceTransforms.size() *
    sizeof(glm::mat4), instanceTransforms.data(), GL_DYNAMIC_DRAW);

    // Enable the attribute location for the transformation matrix
    glEnableVertexAttribArray(2);
    glVertexAttribPointer(2, 4, GL_FLOAT, GL_FALSE,
    sizeof(glm::mat4), (void*)0);
    glEnableVertexAttribArray(3);
    glVertexAttribPointer(3, 4, GL_FLOAT, GL_FALSE,
    sizeof(glm::mat4), (void*)(sizeof(glm::vec4)));
    glEnableVertexAttribArray(4);
    glVertexAttribPointer(4, 4, GL_FLOAT, GL_FALSE,
    sizeof(glm::mat4), (void*)(2 * sizeof(glm::vec4)));
    glEnableVertexAttribArray(5);
    glVertexAttribPointer(5, 4, GL_FLOAT, GL_FALSE,
    sizeof(glm::mat4), (void*)(3 * sizeof(glm::vec4)));

    // Set the divisor for the instance transform attributes
    glVertexAttribDivisor(2, 1);
```

```
    glVertexAttribDivisor(3, 1);
    glVertexAttribDivisor(4, 1);
    glVertexAttribDivisor(5, 1);

    // Issue draw call
    glDrawElementsInstanced(GL_TRIANGLES, object.indexCount,
    GL_UNSIGNED_INT, (void*)(object.startIndex * sizeof(GLuint)),
    instanceTransforms.size());
}
```

Deferred Rendering for Complex Scenes

More accurate lighting calculations are made possible by deferred rendering, which divides the rendering process into multiple passes, particularly in intricate scenarios with plenty of light sources.

Implementation:

```
// Example of deferred rendering using OpenGL
void renderDeferred(const GBuffer& gBuffer, const
std::vector<Light>& lights) {
    // First pass: Geometry pass (fill G-buffer)
    geometryPass();

    // Second pass: Lighting pass
    lightingPass(gBuffer, lights);

    // Third pass: Composite pass
    compositePass(gBuffer);
}
```

Multithreading for Parallelism

Multithreading can be employed to parallelize rendering tasks, such as updating transformations, culling, and issuing draw calls, leading to better CPU utilization.

Implementation:

```cpp
// Example of multithreading for rendering using std::async
#include <future>

std::future<void> renderAsync(const RenderObject& object) {
    return std::async(std::launch::async, [&object] {
        // Render the object asynchronously
        // ...
    });
}
```

Occlusion Culling to Skip Unseen Objects

Occlusion culling involves skipping the rendering of objects that are not visible to the camera, reducing unnecessary rendering computations.

Implementation:

```cpp
// Example of occlusion culling using bounding volumes
bool isObjectVisible(const RenderObject& object, const Camera&
camera) {
    // Perform bounding volume checks (e.g., frustum culling)
    // ...

    return true; // Render object if visible
```

```
}
```

Level of Detail (LOD) Techniques for Performance

Implementing LOD involves using simplified versions of models at different distances from the camera, optimizing rendering performance.

Implementation:

```
// Example of LOD implementation using OpenGL
void renderObjectWithLOD(const RenderObject& object, float
distanceFromCamera) {
    if (distanceFromCamera < LOD_DISTANCE_HIGH) {
        // Render high-detail model
        // ...
    } else if (distanceFromCamera < LOD_DISTANCE_MEDIUM) {
        // Render medium-detail model
        // ...
    } else {
        // Render low-detail model
        // ...
    }
}
```

A key component of high-performance game development is efficient rendering. This section examined methods for maximizing rendering speed in C++ game development, including instanced rendering, deferred rendering, multithreading, occlusion culling, and Level of Detail (LOD). You can make visually striking and responsive gaming experiences for your gamers by carefully using these approaches in accordance with the needs of your game.

GPU optimization strategies

In C++ game programming, GPU optimization is a prerequisite to attaining high-performance graphics rendering. Various techniques to maximize GPU use and enhance overall graphics performance will be covered in this section. Key ideas will be demonstrated with real-world applications and C++ code snippets.

Batching and Instancing for GPU Efficiency

Batching and instancing reduce the number of draw calls sent to the GPU, minimizing CPU overhead and enhancing GPU performance.

Implementation:

```cpp
// Example of GPU-efficient instancing using OpenGL
void renderInstanced(const RenderObject& object, const
std::vector<glm::mat4>& instanceTransforms) {
    // Set common rendering state (shaders, textures, etc.)

    // Set object-specific state (transformation matrix, material
    properties, etc.)

    // Bind VBO for instance transforms
    glBindBuffer(GL_ARRAY_BUFFER, instanceTransformsVBO);
    glBufferData(GL_ARRAY_BUFFER, instanceTransforms.size() *
    sizeof(glm::mat4), instanceTransforms.data(), GL_DYNAMIC_DRAW);

    // Enable the attribute location for the transformation matrix
    glEnableVertexAttribArray(2);
    glVertexAttribPointer(2, 4, GL_FLOAT, GL_FALSE,
    sizeof(glm::mat4), (void*)0);
    glEnableVertexAttribArray(3);
    glVertexAttribPointer(3, 4, GL_FLOAT, GL_FALSE,
    sizeof(glm::mat4), (void*)(sizeof(glm::vec4)));
    glEnableVertexAttribArray(4);
```

```
glVertexAttribPointer(4, 4, GL_FLOAT, GL_FALSE,
sizeof(glm::mat4), (void*)(2 * sizeof(glm::vec4)));
glEnableVertexAttribArray(5);
glVertexAttribPointer(5, 4, GL_FLOAT, GL_FALSE,
sizeof(glm::mat4), (void*)(3 * sizeof(glm::vec4)));

// Set the divisor for the instance transform attributes
glVertexAttribDivisor(2, 1);
glVertexAttribDivisor(3, 1);
glVertexAttribDivisor(4, 1);
glVertexAttribDivisor(5, 1);

// Issue draw call
glDrawElementsInstanced(GL_TRIANGLES, object.indexCount,
GL_UNSIGNED_INT, (void*)(object.startIndex * sizeof(GLuint)),
instanceTransforms.size());
}
```

GPU-Friendly Data Structures

Optimize data structures for efficient GPU processing, minimizing memory access and maximizing parallelism.

Implementation:

```
// Example of GPU-friendly data structure for particles
struct GPUParticle {
    glm::vec3 position;
    glm::vec3 velocity;
    float lifetime;
    // ... additional properties
};
```

Texture Compression for GPU Memory Efficiency

Use texture compression formats to reduce GPU memory usage without sacrificing visual quality.

Implementation:

```
// Example of texture compression using OpenGL
glTexImage2D(GL_TEXTURE_2D, 0, GL_COMPRESSED_RGBA_S3TC_DXT1_EXT,
width, height, 0, GL_RGBA, GL_UNSIGNED_BYTE, data);
```

GPU-Side Culling for Occlusion

Implement GPU-based culling algorithms to skip unnecessary rendering computations for objects not visible to the camera.

Implementation:

```
// Example of GPU-side frustum culling using a compute shader
layout(std430, binding = 0) buffer InBuffer {
    vec4 positions[];
};

layout(std430, binding = 1) buffer OutBuffer {
    int isVisible[];
};

layout (local_size_x = 256, local_size_y = 1, local_size_z = 1) in;

void main() {
    uint index = gl_GlobalInvocationID.x;

    // Perform frustum culling
    isVisible[index] = performFrustumCulling(positions[index]) ? 1
    : 0;
}
```

GPU Resource Management

Efficiently manage GPU resources by reusing existing buffers and textures, minimizing unnecessary allocations and deallocations.

Implementation:

```cpp
// Example of GPU resource management using OpenGL
GLuint createOrUpdateBuffer(const void* data, size_t size, GLuint
existingBuffer = 0) {
    GLuint buffer;
    if (existingBuffer == 0) {
        glGenBuffers(1, &buffer);
    } else {
        buffer = existingBuffer;
    }

    glBindBuffer(GL_ARRAY_BUFFER, buffer);
    glBufferData(GL_ARRAY_BUFFER, size, data, GL_DYNAMIC_DRAW);

    return buffer;
}
```

In C++ game development, GPU optimization techniques are essential to attaining high-performance graphics rendering. To improve GPU efficiency, we've looked into methods like texture compression, batching and instancing, GPU-friendly data structures, GPU-side culling, and GPU resource management. By using these techniques in your game development projects, you'll be able to produce aesthetically striking and fluid games that make the most of contemporary GPU technology.

Enhancing graphics quality while maintaining performance

One of the main challenges in game creation is striking a balance between performance and graphical quality. In C++ game development, this section looks at ways to improve visual quality without sacrificing efficiency.

Shader Techniques for Realistic Lighting

Use sophisticated shader methods, such as Physically Based Rendering (PBR) and Image-Based Lighting (IBL), to improve lighting realism.

Implementation:

```
// Example of a simple PBR shader in HLSL
struct Material {
    float3 albedo;
    float metallic;
    float roughness;
};

float3 PBR(float3 viewDir, float3 normal, float3 lightDir,
Material material) {
    // ... (PBR calculations)
}

// Example of Image-Based Lighting (IBL) in HLSL
float3 IBL(float3 viewDir, float3 normal, Material material) {
    // ... (IBL calculations)
}
```

High-Quality Textures and Materials

Utilize high-quality textures and materials to enhance the visual fidelity of game assets.

Implementation:

```
// Example of loading high-quality textures using OpenGL
GLuint loadTexture(const char* path) {
    // ... (Texture loading code)
    // Ensure the texture has appropriate filtering and mipmapping
    glTexParameteri(GL_TEXTURE_2D, GL_TEXTURE_MIN_FILTER,
    GL_LINEAR_MIPMAP_LINEAR);
    glGenerateMipmap(GL_TEXTURE_2D);
```

```
    return textureID;
}
```

Advanced Anti-Aliasing Techniques

Implement advanced anti-aliasing techniques, such as Temporal Anti-Aliasing (TAA) or Multi-Sample Anti-Aliasing (MSAA), to reduce aliasing artifacts.

Implementation:

```
// Example of enabling MSAA in OpenGL
glfwWindowHint(GLFW_SAMPLES, 4); // 4x MSAA
```

Dynamic Level of Detail (LOD) for Optimized Performance

Implement dynamic LOD techniques to adjust the level of detail based on the camera's distance, optimizing performance without sacrificing visual quality.

Implementation:

```
// Example of dynamic LOD adjustment using OpenGL
void renderObjectWithDynamicLOD(const RenderObject& object, float
distanceFromCamera) {
    float lodFactor = calculateLODFactor(distanceFromCamera);
    adjustObjectLOD(object, lodFactor);
    // ... (Render the object)
}
```

Advanced Post-Processing Effects

Integrate advanced post-processing effects, such as depth of field, motion blur, and screen space reflections, to enhance the overall visual appeal.

Implementation:

```
// Example of enabling screen space reflections in OpenGL
// Requires a screen space reflection shader
glUniform1i(glGetUniformLocation(shaderProgram, "enableSSR"), 1);
```

Efficient Use of GPU Resources

Optimize GPU resource usage by employing efficient data structures and minimizing redundant computations.

Implementation:

```
// Example of using GPU-friendly data structure for particles
struct GPUParticle {
    glm::vec3 position;
    glm::vec3 velocity;
    float lifetime;
    // ... additional properties
};
```

In C++ game development, optimizing visual quality without sacrificing efficiency is a finely balanced task. To accomplish this delicate balance, we looked at methods like sophisticated shader implementations, premium textures, sophisticated anti-aliasing, dynamic LOD, sophisticated post-processing effects, and effective GPU resource management in this section.

Physics and Game Mechanics

Implementing Physics Engines

Introduction to physics engines

In order to provide gaming settings realism and vitality, physics engines are essential. They let developers create realistic collisions, lifelike animations, and captivating gameplay by simulating the physical principles regulating object movement and interaction. This chapter will cover the principles of using physics engines in C++ game programming, along with useful code samples.

Overview of Physics Engines

One piece of software that simulates an object's physical behavior in a virtual world is called a physics engine. It computes the movements and interactions of the game components by considering factors like gravity, friction, and collisions. Physics engines are essential for producing realistic movement, guaranteeing that games follow the rules of physics, and giving interesting gameplay elements a solid base.

Setting Up the Physics Engine Framework

Let's begin by setting up the framework for our basic physics engine. We'll define the fundamental components, including rigid bodies, colliders, and a simple integration method.

```cpp
#include <iostream>
#include <vector>

class RigidBody {
public:
    float mass;
    float position;
    float velocity;
    float force;

    RigidBody(float m, float p, float v) : mass(m), position(p),
    velocity(v), force(0.0f) {}

    void applyForce(float appliedForce) {
        force += appliedForce;
    }

    void update(float deltaTime) {
        // Euler integration
        velocity += (force / mass) * deltaTime;
        position += velocity * deltaTime;

        force = 0.0f;  // Reset force for the next frame
    }
};

int main() {
    // Create a rigid body
    RigidBody object(1.0f, 0.0f, 0.0f);

    // Simulation loop
    for (float time = 0.0f; time < 5.0f; time += 0.1f) {
        object.applyForce(9.8f);  // Apply gravity
        object.update(0.1f);      // Update object's position
        based on simulation time step

        std::cout << "Time: " << time << "s, Position: " <<
        object.position << "m\n";
```

```
    }

    return 0;
}
```

In this initial example, we've defined a simple **RigidBody** class representing an object with mass, position, velocity, and force. The simulation loop applies a gravitational force, and the object's position is updated using Euler integration.

Introducing Colliders for Collision Detection

Now, let's enhance our physics engine by introducing basic colliders and implementing collision detection between two rigid bodies.

```cpp
#include <iostream>
#include <vector>

class Collider {
public:
    float position;

    Collider(float p) : position(p) {}
};

class RigidBody {
public:
    float mass;
    float position;
    float velocity;
    float force;
    Collider collider;

    RigidBody(float m, float p, float v) : mass(m), position(p),
    velocity(v), force(0.0f), collider(p) {}
```

```cpp
    void applyForce(float appliedForce) {
        force += appliedForce;
    }

    void update(float deltaTime) {
        velocity += (force / mass) * deltaTime;
        position += velocity * deltaTime;
        force = 0.0f;  // Reset force for the next frame
    }
};

bool checkCollision(const RigidBody& obj1, const RigidBody& obj2) {
    // Check if the distance between colliders is less than a
    collision threshold
    return std::abs(obj1.collider.position -
    obj2.collider.position) < 0.1f;
}

int main() {
    // Create two rigid bodies with colliders
    RigidBody object1(1.0f, 0.0f, 0.0f);
    RigidBody object2(1.0f, 2.0f, 0.0f);

    // Simulation loop
    for (float time = 0.0f; time < 5.0f; time += 0.1f) {
        object1.applyForce(9.8f);  // Apply gravity to the first
        object
        object1.update(0.1f);

        object2.applyForce(9.8f);  // Apply gravity to the second
        object
        object2.update(0.1f);

        if (checkCollision(object1, object2)) {
            std::cout << "Collision detected at time: " << time <<
            "s\n";
        }
    }

    return 0;
```

```
}
```

In this extended example, each **RigidBody** now contains a **Collider**, and the **checkCollision** function determines whether two objects are colliding based on the distance between their colliders.

Integrating physics into game development

We'll look at how to include physics into C++ game programming in this section. The main goal will be to integrate a physics engine into a game framework so that game designers may design realistic and dynamic interactions between different game elements. The integration process will be demonstrated with real-world C++ code examples throughout this section.

Selecting a Physics Engine Library

Before diving into the integration process, it's essential to choose a physics engine library that suits your game development needs. Popular physics engine libraries for C++ include:

1. **Box2D:** A lightweight 2D physics engine suitable for games with 2D graphics.
2. **Bullet Physics:** A versatile 3D physics engine supporting rigid body dynamics, soft body dynamics, and more.
3. **Newton Dynamics:** A physics engine that excels in simulating complex interactions and supports both 2D and 3D environments.

For this section, we'll demonstrate the integration process using Box2D, a widely-used 2D physics engine.

Setting Up Box2D for Integration

First, you need to download and set up Box2D in your C++ project. Below is a simplified example of setting up Box2D using a package manager like vcpkg:

```
# Install Box2D using vcpkg
vcpkg install box2d
```

Now, let's create a simple C++ program that integrates Box2D into a game framework.

```cpp
#include <iostream>
#include <Box2D/Box2D.h>

class MyContactListener : public b2ContactListener {
public:
    void BeginContact(b2Contact* contact) override {
        std::cout << "Collision detected!" << std::endl;
    }
};

int main() {
    // Set up Box2D world
    b2Vec2 gravity(0.0f, -9.8f);
    b2World world(gravity);

    // Create ground body
    b2BodyDef groundBodyDef;
    groundBodyDef.position.Set(0.0f, -10.0f);
    b2Body* groundBody = world.CreateBody(&groundBodyDef);

    b2PolygonShape groundBox;
    groundBox.SetAsBox(50.0f, 10.0f);
    groundBody->CreateFixture(&groundBox, 0.0f);

    // Create dynamic body
    b2BodyDef dynamicBodyDef;
    dynamicBodyDef.type = b2_dynamicBody;
    dynamicBodyDef.position.Set(0.0f, 4.0f);
    b2Body* dynamicBody = world.CreateBody(&dynamicBodyDef);
```

```cpp
    b2PolygonShape dynamicBox;
    dynamicBox.SetAsBox(1.0f, 1.0f);

    b2FixtureDef fixtureDef;
    fixtureDef.shape = &dynamicBox;
    fixtureDef.density = 1.0f;
    fixtureDef.friction = 0.3f;

    dynamicBody->CreateFixture(&fixtureDef);

    // Set up contact listener
    MyContactListener contactListener;
    world.SetContactListener(&contactListener);

    // Simulation loop
    for (int32_t i = 0; i < 60; ++i) {
        world.Step(1.0f / 60.0f, 6, 2);
    }

    return 0;
}
```

In this example, we've set up a simple Box2D world with a ground and a
dynamic box. The **MyContactListener** class is a custom contact listener that
prints a message when collisions occur.

Incorporating Physics with Game Entities

Let's now incorporate physics into a game framework using virtual characters.
The integration procedure will involve updating the game entities depending
on the physics simulation, using a hypothetical game framework.

```cpp
#include <iostream>
#include <Box2D/Box2D.h>

class GameObject {
public:
```

```cpp
    b2Body* body;

    GameObject(b2World& world, float x, float y) {
        b2BodyDef bodyDef;
        bodyDef.type = b2_dynamicBody;
        bodyDef.position.Set(x, y);
        body = world.CreateBody(&bodyDef);

        b2PolygonShape dynamicBox;
        dynamicBox.SetAsBox(1.0f, 1.0f);

        b2FixtureDef fixtureDef;
        fixtureDef.shape = &dynamicBox;
        fixtureDef.density = 1.0f;
        fixtureDef.friction = 0.3f;

        body->CreateFixture(&fixtureDef);
    }

    void update() {
        // Update game entity based on physics simulation
        std::cout << "Entity Position: (" << body->GetPosition().x
        << ", " << body->GetPosition().y << ")\n";
    }
};

int main() {
    // Set up Box2D world
    b2Vec2 gravity(0.0f, -9.8f);
    b2World world(gravity);

    // Create game entity
    GameObject entity(world, 0.0f, 4.0f);

    // Simulation loop
    for (int32_t i = 0; i < 60; ++i) {
        world.Step(1.0f / 60.0f, 6, 2);

        // Update game entities
        entity.update();
```

```
    }

    return 0;
}
```

In this example, the **GameObject** class represents a game entity with a Box2D body. The simulation loop updates both the physics world and the game entities.

Creating dynamic and interactive game experiences is made possible by integrating physics into C++ game development. We used the Box2D physics engine to explain the integration process in this section. You'll be able to give your game environments realism and involvement when you include physics into your projects.

Simulating realistic game environments

One of the most important aspects of game production that significantly enhances player immersion is the creation of realistic game worlds. This section focuses on creating realistic surroundings in C++ game development by utilizing a variety of methods and tools. Realistic C++ code samples will be used to demonstrate how to achieve realism in various gaming environment characteristics throughout this section.

Realistic Terrain Generation

Realistic terrain generation is crucial for games that take place in large, varied settings. To generate landscapes that appear natural, one common approach for procedural terrain synthesis is perlin noise.

```
#include <iostream>
#include <cmath>
```

```cpp
// Perlin noise function
float perlin(float x, float y) {
    // Implementation of Perlin noise (omitted for brevity)
    // ...

    return 0.0f;  // Placeholder, replace with actual
    implementation
}

// Terrain generation function using Perlin noise
void generateTerrain() {
    const int width = 100;
    const int height = 100;

    for (int y = 0; y < height; ++y) {
        for (int x = 0; x < width; ++x) {
            float terrainHeight = perlin(x * 0.1f, y * 0.1f) *
            10.0f;
            std::cout << terrainHeight << " ";
        }
        std::cout << "\n";
    }
}

int main() {
    generateTerrain();

    return 0;
}
```

In this example, a simplified Perlin noise function is used to generate terrain heights. Adjust the parameters to achieve different terrains and landscapes.

Realistic Water Simulation

Simulating realistic water is crucial for games featuring bodies of water. The Smoothed Particle Hydrodynamics (SPH) algorithm is commonly used for fluid simulation.

```cpp
#include <iostream>

class WaterParticle {
public:
    float x, y;
    float velocityX, velocityY;

    WaterParticle(float posX, float posY) : x(posX), y(posY),
    velocityX(0.0f), velocityY(0.0f) {}
};

class WaterSimulation {
private:
    static const int numParticles = 100;

public:
    WaterParticle particles[numParticles];

    void simulate(float deltaTime) {
        // SPH fluid simulation (omitted for brevity)
        // ...

        // Placeholder: Update particle positions and velocities
        for (int i = 0; i < numParticles; ++i) {
            particles[i].x += particles[i].velocityX * deltaTime;
            particles[i].y += particles[i].velocityY * deltaTime;
        }
    }
};

int main() {
    WaterSimulation waterSim;

    // Simulation loop
    for (int i = 0; i < 60; ++i) {
        waterSim.simulate(0.1f);

        // Rendering code (omitted for brevity)
```

```
        // ...
    }

    return 0;
}
```

Using the SPH technique, a water simulation is represented simply in this example. To see the water in your game, change the parameters and add rendering code.

Dynamic Weather Systems

Adding dynamic weather systems to game environments makes them more realistic. Particle systems and environmental effects can be adjusted to simulate meteorological occurrences, such as rain or snow.

```
#include <iostream>

class Particle {
public:
    float x, y;
    float velocityX, velocityY;

    Particle(float posX, float posY) : x(posX), y(posY),
    velocityX(0.0f), velocityY(0.0f) {}
};

class WeatherSystem {
private:
    static const int numParticles = 100;

public:
    Particle particles[numParticles];

    void simulateRain(float deltaTime) {
        // Simulate rain particle motion (omitted for brevity)
```

```cpp
        // ...

        // Placeholder: Update particle positions and velocities
        for (int i = 0; i < numParticles; ++i) {
            particles[i].x += particles[i].velocityX * deltaTime;
            particles[i].y += particles[i].velocityY * deltaTime;
        }
    }
};

int main() {
    WeatherSystem rainSystem;

    // Simulation loop
    for (int i = 0; i < 60; ++i) {
        rainSystem.simulateRain(0.1f);

        // Rendering code (omitted for brevity)
        // ...
    }

    return 0;
}
```

This example demonstrates a simple rain simulation using particle motion. Integrate this with your game's rendering system to create a dynamic weather experience.

Day-Night Cycle

Implementing a day-night cycle adds realism to game environments. Adjusting lighting and sky color based on the time of day creates a dynamic and immersive atmosphere.

```cpp
#include <iostream>
```

```cpp
class DayNightCycle {
private:
    float timeOfDay; // Range: 0.0 (midnight) to 1.0 (midnight of
    the next day)

public:
    DayNightCycle() : timeOfDay(0.0f) {}

    void updateTime(float deltaTime) {
        // Increment time based on game speed
        timeOfDay += 0.01f * deltaTime;

        // Wrap around to simulate a 24-hour day
        if (timeOfDay > 1.0f) {
            timeOfDay -= 1.0f;
        }
    }

    void updateEnvironment() {
        // Adjust lighting, sky color, and other environmental
        factors based on time of day
        // ...

        std::cout << "Time of Day: " << timeOfDay << "\n";
    }
};

int main() {
    DayNightCycle dayNightCycle;

    // Simulation loop
    for (int i = 0; i < 60; ++i) {
        dayNightCycle.updateTime(0.1f);
        dayNightCycle.updateEnvironment();

        // Rendering code (omitted for brevity)
        // ...
    }

    return 0;
```

```
}
```

In this example, the **DayNightCycle** class updates the time of day and adjusts environmental factors accordingly. Integrate this with your game's rendering and lighting systems to create a convincing day-night cycle.

Using a variety of approaches, including dynamic weather systems, water simulation, day-night cycles, and terrain generation, is necessary to create realistic gaming landscapes in C++ game development. These components all work together to create compelling and immersive gaming environments. Take into account the particular needs of your game when you include these characteristics into your work, and modify the simulations to get the desired degree of realism.

Game Mechanics and Interactivity

Any game's core is its interaction and game mechanics, which determine how the player feels and how involved they are. This chapter delves into utilizing C++ to implement game mechanics. We'll look at how to develop dynamic and interactive gameplay features using real-world examples and snippets of code.

Player Input Handling

Reactive and interactive game development requires effectively managing player input. A variety of libraries and methods for gathering and handling user input are available in C++. Here's a basic example of managing keyboard input with the SFML library:

```cpp
#include <SFML/Graphics.hpp>

int main() {
    sf::RenderWindow window(sf::VideoMode(800, 600), "Player Input
    Example");

    while (window.isOpen()) {
        sf::Event event;
        while (window.pollEvent(event)) {
            if (event.type == sf::Event::Closed) {
                window.close();
            }
```

```cpp
        // Handle keyboard input
        if (event.type == sf::Event::KeyPressed) {
            if (event.key.code == sf::Keyboard::Left) {
                // Handle left arrow key
            } else if (event.key.code == sf::Keyboard::Right) {
                // Handle right arrow key
            }
        }
    }

    // Game update and rendering (omitted for brevity)
    // ...
}

    return 0;
}
```

In this example, SFML is used to create a window and handle keyboard input. Adjust the code to accommodate your specific input requirements.

Character Movement and Animation

Implementing character movement and animation is essential for bringing game worlds to life. Consider the following example using a simple character class:

```cpp
#include <SFML/Graphics.hpp>

class Character {
private:
    sf::Sprite sprite;
    sf::Texture texture;
    float speed;

public:
    Character() : speed(200.0f) {
        if (!texture.loadFromFile("character.png")) {
```

```cpp
            // Handle texture loading error
        }

        sprite.setTexture(texture);
        sprite.setPosition(400.0f, 300.0f);
    }

    void move(sf::Vector2f direction, float deltaTime) {
        sprite.move(direction * speed * deltaTime);
    }

    void draw(sf::RenderWindow& window) {
        window.draw(sprite);
    }
};

int main() {
    sf::RenderWindow window(sf::VideoMode(800, 600), "Character
    Movement Example");

    Character player;

    while (window.isOpen()) {
        sf::Event event;
        while (window.pollEvent(event)) {
            if (event.type == sf::Event::Closed) {
                window.close();
            }
        }

        // Handle player input for movement
        sf::Vector2f movement(0.0f, 0.0f);
        if (sf::Keyboard::isKeyPressed(sf::Keyboard::Left)) {
            movement.x = -1.0f;
        } else if
        (sf::Keyboard::isKeyPressed(sf::Keyboard::Right)) {
            movement.x = 1.0f;
        }

        player.move(movement, 0.1f);
```

```cpp
        // Game update and rendering
        window.clear();
        player.draw(window);
        window.display();
    }

    return 0;
}
```

In this example, a **Character** class encapsulates the character's properties and behavior. The character responds to left and right arrow key inputs, moving accordingly.

Implementing Game Logic and Rules

Game mechanics often involve implementing rules and logic that govern the game's behavior. Let's consider a simple example of a player collecting items and scoring points:

```cpp
#include <SFML/Graphics.hpp>

class Player {
private:
    sf::Sprite sprite;
    sf::Texture texture;
    int score;

public:
    Player() : score(0) {
        if (!texture.loadFromFile("player.png")) {
            // Handle texture loading error
        }

        sprite.setTexture(texture);
        sprite.setPosition(400.0f, 300.0f);
```

```cpp
    }

    void collectItem() {
        score += 10;
    }

    int getScore() const {
        return score;
    }

    void draw(sf::RenderWindow& window) {
        window.draw(sprite);
    }
};

class Item {
private:
    sf::Sprite sprite;
    sf::Texture texture;

public:
    Item(float x, float y) {
        if (!texture.loadFromFile("item.png")) {
            // Handle texture loading error
        }

        sprite.setTexture(texture);
        sprite.setPosition(x, y);
    }

    sf::Vector2f getPosition() const {
        return sprite.getPosition();
    }

    void draw(sf::RenderWindow& window) {
        window.draw(sprite);
    }
};

int main() {
```

```cpp
sf::RenderWindow window(sf::VideoMode(800, 600), "Game Logic
Example");

Player player;
Item item(200.0f, 200.0f);

while (window.isOpen()) {
    sf::Event event;
    while (window.pollEvent(event)) {
        if (event.type == sf::Event::Closed) {
            window.close();
        }
    }


    // Check for item collection
    if (sf::Keyboard::isKeyPressed(sf::Keyboard::Space)) {
        sf::Vector2f playerPos = player.getPosition();
        sf::Vector2f itemPos = item.getPosition();

        float distance = std::sqrt((playerPos.x - itemPos.x) *
        (playerPos.x - itemPos.x) +
                                    (playerPos.y - itemPos.y) *
                                    (playerPos.y - itemPos.y));

        if (distance < 50.0f) {
            player.collectItem();
            item = Item(rand() % 700 + 50, rand() % 500 + 50);
            // Move item to a new random position
        }
    }


    // Game update and rendering
    window.clear();
    player.draw(window);
    item.draw(window);
    window.display();

    std::cout << "Score: " << player.getScore() << "\n";
}
```

```
    return 0;
}
```

In this example, the player can collect items by pressing the space key. The player's score increases upon successful collection, and a new item appears at a random position.

Interactivity and game mechanics are essential elements that characterize a game's core. We investigated utilizing C++ to handle player input, create character movement and animation, and add game logic and rules. Think about the distinctive mechanics that will add to the game's replay value and player engagement as you design it.

Creating interactive game elements

Developing interactive game features is essential to producing engaging gameplay. This section explores the use of C++ to construct several interactive features. Creating dynamic and engaging features for your games will be made easier with the help of real-world examples and code snippets.

Interactive Buttons and Menus

User interfaces often include interactive elements like buttons and menus. The following example showcases a basic button class using SFML:

```cpp
#include <SFML/Graphics.hpp>

class Button {
private:
    sf::RectangleShape shape;
    sf::Text text;
    sf::Font font;
```

```cpp
public:
    Button(float x, float y, float width, float height,
    std::string buttonText)
        : shape(sf::Vector2f(width, height)), text(buttonText,
        font) {
        shape.setPosition(x, y);
        shape.setFillColor(sf::Color::Blue);

        font.loadFromFile("arial.ttf");
        text.setFont(font);
        text.setCharacterSize(20);
        text.setFillColor(sf::Color::White);

        // Center the text within the button
        sf::FloatRect textBounds = text.getLocalBounds();
        text.setPosition(x + (width - textBounds.width) / 2, y +
        (height - textBounds.height) / 2);
    }

    void draw(sf::RenderWindow& window) {
        window.draw(shape);
        window.draw(text);
    }

    bool isMouseOver(sf::RenderWindow& window) const {
        sf::Vector2f mousePos =
        sf::Vector2f(sf::Mouse::getPosition(window));
        return shape.getGlobalBounds().contains(mousePos);
    }
};

int main() {
    sf::RenderWindow window(sf::VideoMode(800, 600), "Button
    Example");

    Button playButton(200.0f, 200.0f, 120.0f, 50.0f, "Play");

    while (window.isOpen()) {
        sf::Event event;
```

```cpp
        while (window.pollEvent(event)) {
            if (event.type == sf::Event::Closed) {
                window.close();
            }

            // Check for button click
            if (event.type == sf::Event::MouseButtonPressed &&
            event.mouseButton.button == sf::Mouse::Left) {
                if (playButton.isMouseOver(window)) {
                    std::cout << "Play button clicked!\n";
                }
            }
        }

        window.clear();
        playButton.draw(window);
        window.display();
    }

    return 0;
}
```

This example demonstrates a basic button class with features like positioning, sizing, and mouse interaction.

Interactive Physics Objects

Integrating physics into interactive objects adds a layer of realism and engagement. The following example uses Box2D to create a draggable physics object:

```cpp
#include <SFML/Graphics.hpp>
#include <Box2D/Box2D.h>

class PhysicsObject {
private:
    b2Body* body;
```

```cpp
    sf::RectangleShape shape;

public:
    PhysicsObject(b2World& world, float x, float y, float width,
    float height)
        : shape(sf::Vector2f(width, height)) {
        b2BodyDef bodyDef;
        bodyDef.type = b2_dynamicBody;
        bodyDef.position.Set(x, y);
        body = world.CreateBody(&bodyDef);

        b2PolygonShape dynamicBox;
        dynamicBox.SetAsBox(width / 2.0f, height / 2.0f);

        b2FixtureDef fixtureDef;
        fixtureDef.shape = &dynamicBox;
        fixtureDef.density = 1.0f;
        fixtureDef.friction = 0.3f;

        body->CreateFixture(&fixtureDef);

        shape.setPosition(x - width / 2.0f, y - height / 2.0f);
        shape.setFillColor(sf::Color::Green);
    }

    void draw(sf::RenderWindow& window) {
        shape.setPosition(body->GetPosition().x -
        shape.getSize().x / 2.0f,
                          body->GetPosition().y -
                          shape.getSize().y / 2.0f);
        window.draw(shape);
    }

    void drag(sf::Vector2f mousePos) {
        b2Vec2 targetPos(mousePos.x, mousePos.y);
        body->SetTransform(targetPos, 0.0f);
    }
};

int main() {
```

```cpp
    sf::RenderWindow window(sf::VideoMode(800, 600), "Physics
    Object Example");

    b2Vec2 gravity(0.0f, 9.8f);
    b2World world(gravity);

    PhysicsObject physicsObject(world, 400.0f, 300.0f, 50.0f,
    50.0f);

    while (window.isOpen()) {
        sf::Event event;
        while (window.pollEvent(event)) {
            if (event.type == sf::Event::Closed) {
                window.close();
            }

            // Check for mouse drag
            if (event.type == sf::Event::MouseButtonPressed &&
            event.mouseButton.button == sf::Mouse::Left) {
                sf::Vector2f mousePos =
                sf::Vector2f(sf::Mouse::getPosition(window));
                physicsObject.drag(mousePos);
            }
        }

        // Simulate physics
        world.Step(1.0f / 60.0f, 6, 2);

        window.clear();
        physicsObject.draw(window);
        window.display();
    }

    return 0;
}
```

In this example, the **PhysicsObject** class uses Box2D to create a dynamic physics object that can be dragged by the mouse.

Interactive Game Events

Adding interactive events to your game keeps players engaged. The following example demonstrates a simple event system using observers:

```cpp
#include <iostream>
#include <vector>

class EventObserver {
public:
    virtual void onEvent() = 0;
};

class InteractiveElement {
private:
    std::vector<EventObserver*> observers;

public:
    void addObserver(EventObserver* observer) {
        observers.push_back(observer);
    }

    void notifyObservers() {
        for (EventObserver* observer : observers) {
            observer->onEvent();
        }
    }

    void interact() {
        std::cout << "Interactive element clicked!\n";
        notifyObservers();
    }
};

class ScoreObserver : public EventObserver {
public:
    void onEvent() override {
        std::cout << "Score increased!\n";
    }
};

int main() {
```

```cpp
    InteractiveElement interactiveElement;

    // Create observers
    ScoreObserver scoreObserver1;
    ScoreObserver scoreObserver2;

    // Add observers to the interactive element
    interactiveElement.addObserver(&scoreObserver1);
    interactiveElement.addObserver(&scoreObserver2);

    // Simulate interaction
    interactiveElement.interact();

    return 0;
}
```

In this example, the **InteractiveElement** class has an observer pattern. When the element is interacted with, it notifies its observers, triggering specific actions.

A combination of event-driven programming, physics integration, and user interface design goes into making interactive game pieces. We looked at physics-driven objects, interactive menus and buttons, and game events. Take into account the distinct gaming experiences you hope to provide as you integrate these components into your games.

Implementing game mechanics using C++

Creating interactions, rules, and other frameworks that influence the player's experience is the process of putting your game concept into practice. This section looks at real-world instances of utilizing C++ to implement different game concepts. To learn how to effectively develop and implement these mechanics, let's delve into the code.

Health and Damage System

A fundamental game mechanic is the health and damage system. This example illustrates a simple implementation using a **Player** class:

```cpp
#include <iostream>

class Player {
private:
    int health;

public:
    Player(int initialHealth) : health(initialHealth) {}

    void takeDamage(int damage) {
        health -= damage;
        if (health <= 0) {
            std::cout << "Player defeated!\n";
        } else {
            std::cout << "Player health: " << health << "\n";
        }
    }

    void heal(int amount) {
        health += amount;
        std::cout << "Player healed. Health: " << health << "\n";
    }
};

int main() {
    Player player(100);

    // Simulate game events
    player.takeDamage(20);
    player.takeDamage(50);
    player.heal(30);
    player.takeDamage(80);

    return 0;
}
```

In this example, the **Player** class includes functions for taking damage and healing. Adjust the initial health and damage values according to your game's balance.

Inventory System

An inventory system is crucial for games with items and resources. Here's a basic implementation using a **PlayerInventory** class:

```cpp
#include <iostream>
#include <vector>
#include <string>

class Item {
public:
    std::string name;

    Item(const std::string& itemName) : name(itemName) {}
};

class PlayerInventory {
private:
    std::vector<Item> items;

public:
    void addItem(const Item& item) {
        items.push_back(item);
        std::cout << "Added item: " << item.name << "\n";
    }

    void listItems() const {
        std::cout << "Inventory Items:\n";
        for (const Item& item : items) {
            std::cout << "- " << item.name << "\n";
        }
    }
};

int main() {
```

```cpp
    PlayerInventory inventory;

    // Simulate game events
    Item sword("Iron Sword");
    Item potion("Health Potion");

    inventory.addItem(sword);
    inventory.addItem(potion);

    inventory.listItems();

    return 0;
}
```

In this example, the **PlayerInventory** class allows adding items and listing the current inventory. Extend this system to include item usage and interactions.

Quest System

Implementing a quest system adds depth and progression to your game. Here's a basic representation using a **Quest** class:

```cpp
#include <iostream>
#include <string>

class Quest {
private:
    std::string description;
    bool isCompleted;

public:
    Quest(const std::string& questDescription) :
    description(questDescription), isCompleted(false) {}

    void complete() {
        isCompleted = true;
        std::cout << "Quest completed: " << description << "\n";
```

```cpp
    }

    bool isQuestCompleted() const {
        return isCompleted;
    }
};

class Player {
private:
    Quest activeQuest;

public:
    void startQuest(const Quest& quest) {
        activeQuest = quest;
        std::cout << "Quest started: " << quest.getDescription()
        << "\n";
    }

    void checkQuestStatus() const {
        if (activeQuest.isQuestCompleted()) {
            std::cout << "Current quest is completed!\n";
        } else {
            std::cout << "Current quest is in progress.\n";
        }
    }
};

int main() {
    Quest defeatEnemies("Defeat 10 Enemies");
    Quest findArtifact("Find the Ancient Artifact");

    Player player;
    player.startQuest(defeatEnemies);

    // Simulate game events
    player.checkQuestStatus();
    defeatEnemies.complete();
    player.checkQuestStatus();

    return 0;
```

```
    }
```

In this example, the **Quest** class represents individual quests, and the **Player** class interacts with the quest system by starting and checking quest status.

User input handling and event-driven programming

Interactive games require both event–driven programming and user participation. This section looks at how to create event–driven systems in C++ and manage user input efficiently. Creating dynamic and responsive gameplay experiences is made easier with the help of real–world examples and code snippets.

Handling Keyboard Input

Capturing and processing keyboard input is fundamental for player interaction. The following example illustrates how to handle keyboard input using SFML:

```cpp
#include <SFML/Graphics.hpp>

int main() {
    sf::RenderWindow window(sf::VideoMode(800, 600), "Keyboard
    Input Example");

    while (window.isOpen()) {
        sf::Event event;
        while (window.pollEvent(event)) {
            if (event.type == sf::Event::Closed) {
                window.close();
            }

            // Handle keyboard input
            if (event.type == sf::Event::KeyPressed) {
                if (event.key.code == sf::Keyboard::W) {
                    // Handle 'W' key press
                } else if (event.key.code == sf::Keyboard::A) {
```

```
                    // Handle 'A' key press
                } else if (event.key.code == sf::Keyboard::S) {
                    // Handle 'S' key press
                } else if (event.key.code == sf::Keyboard::D) {
                    // Handle 'D' key press
                }
            }
        }

        // Game update and rendering (omitted for brevity)
        // ...

        window.clear();
        // Draw game elements
        window.display();
    }

    return 0;
}
```

In this example, the program responds to the key presses of 'W,' 'A,' 'S,' and 'D'. Modify the code to fit the specific controls of your game.

Mouse Input Handling

Processing mouse input is crucial for games that require pointing and clicking. The following code snippet demonstrates how to handle mouse input using SFML:

```
#include <SFML/Graphics.hpp>

int main() {
    sf::RenderWindow window(sf::VideoMode(800, 600), "Mouse Input
    Example");

    while (window.isOpen()) {
```

```cpp
    sf::Event event;
    while (window.pollEvent(event)) {
        if (event.type == sf::Event::Closed) {
            window.close();
        }

        // Handle mouse input
        if (event.type == sf::Event::MouseButtonPressed) {
            if (event.mouseButton.button == sf::Mouse::Left) {
                // Handle left mouse button click
            } else if (event.mouseButton.button ==
            sf::Mouse::Right) {
                // Handle right mouse button click
            }
        }

        // Handle mouse movement
        if (event.type == sf::Event::MouseMoved) {
            // Get mouse coordinates: event.mouseMove.x,
            event.mouseMove.y
            // Handle mouse movement
        }
    }

    // Game update and rendering (omitted for brevity)
    // ...

    window.clear();
    // Draw game elements
    window.display();
}

return 0;
}
```

This example responds to left and right mouse button clicks as well as mouse movement. Adjust the code based on your game's mouse input requirements.

Event-Driven Programming with Observers

Implementing an event-driven system using observers allows for modular and decoupled code. The following example showcases a basic implementation:

```cpp
#include <iostream>
#include <vector>

class EventObserver {
public:
    virtual void onEvent() = 0;
};

class EventHandler {
private:
    std::vector<EventObserver*> observers;

public:
    void addObserver(EventObserver* observer) {
        observers.push_back(observer);
    }

    void notifyObservers() {
        for (EventObserver* observer : observers) {
            observer->onEvent();
        }
    }

    void simulateEvent() {
        std::cout << "Event occurred!\n";
        notifyObservers();
    }
};

class ExampleObserver : public EventObserver {
public:
    void onEvent() override {
        std::cout << "ExampleObserver received the event!\n";
    }
};

int main() {
```

```cpp
    EventHandler eventHandler;
    ExampleObserver exampleObserver;

    // Add observer to the event handler
    eventHandler.addObserver(&exampleObserver);

    // Simulate an event
    eventHandler.simulateEvent();

    return 0;
}
```

In this example, the **EventObserver** class defines the interface for observers, and the **EventHandler** class manages the observers and notifies them when an event occurs.

User input handling and event-driven programming are essential for creating interactive and dynamic gameplay experiences in C++ game development.

Audio and AI Integration

Audio Integration in C++

Your game needs audio if you want to make it immersive and interesting. The integration of audio features into your C++ game is covered in this chapter. You will be guided through the implementation of various audio features with the use of real-world examples and code snippets.

Playing Sound Effects

Playing sound effects enhances the overall atmosphere of your game. The following example demonstrates how to use SFML to play a sound effect:

```cpp
#include <SFML/Audio.hpp>

int main() {
    sf::SoundBuffer buffer;
    if (!buffer.loadFromFile("sound_effect.wav")) {
        // Handle loading error
        return -1;
    }

    sf::Sound sound;
    sound.setBuffer(buffer);

    // Play the sound effect
    sound.play();

    // Wait for the sound to finish (optional)
```

```cpp
    while (sound.getStatus() == sf::Sound::Playing) {
        // Keep the program running
    }

    return 0;
}
```

In this example, replace "sound_effect.wav" with the actual path to your sound effect file. SFML provides various features for controlling the playback, volume, and pitch of the sound.

Background Music

Background music sets the tone for your game. The following code snippet demonstrates how to play background music using SFML:

```cpp
#include <SFML/Audio.hpp>

int main() {
    sf::Music music;
    if (!music.openFromFile("background_music.ogg")) {
        // Handle loading error
        return -1;
    }

    // Play the background music
    music.play();

    // Keep the program running to allow background music playback
    while (true) {
        // Your game logic here
    }

    return 0;
}
```

Similar to the previous example, replace "background_music.ogg" with the path to your background music file. SFML's **Music** class provides features for controlling music playback, volume, pitch, and more.

Implementing Sound Effects in Game Events

Integrating sound effects into specific game events adds depth and feedback. The following example demonstrates how to play a sound effect in response to a game event:

```cpp
#include <SFML/Audio.hpp>

class GameEvent {
public:
    virtual void trigger() = 0;
};

class SoundEffectEvent : public GameEvent {
private:
    sf::SoundBuffer buffer;
    sf::Sound sound;

public:
    SoundEffectEvent(const std::string& soundFilePath) {
        if (!buffer.loadFromFile(soundFilePath)) {
            // Handle loading error
        }

        sound.setBuffer(buffer);
    }

    void trigger() override {
        sound.play();
    }
};

int main() {
    SoundEffectEvent explosionEvent("explosion.wav");

    // Simulate a game event
```

```
    explosionEvent.trigger();

    // Keep the program running to allow sound effect playback
    while (true) {
        // Your game logic here
    }

    return 0;
}
```

In this example, the **SoundEffectEvent** class is triggered to play a sound effect. Adjust the file path and integrate similar events into your game logic.

Sound systems and libraries

Developing a powerful audio system is crucial to producing a captivating gaming environment. This part examines C++ sound libraries and systems with an emphasis on adding sophisticated features to your game. Using well-known C++ audio libraries, you will be guided through the implementation of a sound system with the help of useful examples and code snippets.

Introduction to Advanced Sound Systems

Beyond basic playback, advanced sound systems include capabilities like dynamic mixing, spatial audio, and real-time effects. This section defines the essential elements of an advanced sound system and presents the idea of one.

Spatial Audio

The way sound behaves in three dimensions is simulated by spatial audio. It enables the placement of sounds in a virtual setting, giving the player a more lifelike auditory experience.

Dynamic Mixing

Dynamic mixing involves adjusting the volume, pitch, and other parameters of multiple sound sources in real-time. This allows for seamless transitions and layering of audio elements.

Real-time Effects

Real-time effects, such as reverb or echo, enhance the audio experience by applying changes to the sound in real-time based on the virtual environment or specific game events.

Integrating Advanced Sound Systems with OpenAL

Cross-platform audio API OpenAL allows for dynamic mixing and spatial audio. An example of a simple OpenAL implementation of an advanced sound system is provided below:

```cpp
#include <AL/al.h>
#include <AL/alc.h>

int main() {
    // Initialize OpenAL context and device
    ALCdevice* device = alcOpenDevice(nullptr);
    ALCcontext* context = alcCreateContext(device, nullptr);
    alcMakeContextCurrent(context);

    // Create a sound buffer and source
    ALuint buffer, source;
    alGenBuffers(1, &buffer);
    alGenSources(1, &source);

    // Load sound data into the buffer (replace "sound_data.wav"
    with your file)
    // Use a sound library or a custom loader for different formats
    // For simplicity, we assume a WAV file in this example
```

```cpp
// ...

// Attach the buffer to the source
alSourcei(source, AL_BUFFER, buffer);

// Set source properties (position, volume, etc.) for spatial
audio
// ...

// Play the sound
alSourcePlay(source);

// Wait for the sound to finish (optional)
ALint sourceState;
do {
    alGetSourcei(source, AL_SOURCE_STATE, &sourceState);
} while (sourceState == AL_PLAYING);

// Cleanup resources
alDeleteSources(1, &source);
alDeleteBuffers(1, &buffer);
alcMakeContextCurrent(nullptr);
alcDestroyContext(context);
alcCloseDevice(device);

return 0;
}
```

In this example, replace "sound_data.wav" with the path to your sound file. This code sets up an OpenAL context, creates a sound buffer and source, loads sound data, and plays the sound with basic spatial audio properties.

Utilizing FMOD Studio for Advanced Sound Systems

Advanced sound design and execution are supported by FMOD Studio, a professional-grade audio authoring tool. How to include FMOD Studio into a C++ game is demonstrated in the example below:

```cpp
#include <fmod.hpp>

int main() {
    FMOD::System* system;
    FMOD::Sound* sound;
    FMOD::Channel* channel;

    // Create the main system object
    FMOD::System_Create(&system);
    system->init(32, FMOD_INIT_NORMAL, nullptr);

    // Load and play a sound (replace "sound_data.mp3" with your
    file)
    // Use FMOD Studio for more advanced sound design
    system->createSound("sound_data.mp3", FMOD_DEFAULT, nullptr,
    &sound);
    system->playSound(sound, nullptr, false, &channel);

    // Wait for the sound to finish (optional)
    channel->isPlaying(&isPlaying);
    while (isPlaying) {
        // Keep the program running
        channel->isPlaying(&isPlaying);
    }

    // Release resources
    sound->release();
    system->close();
    system->release();

    return 0;
}
```

In this example, replace "sound_data.mp3" with the path to your sound
file. FMOD Studio provides a comprehensive environment for designing and
implementing advanced sound systems.

Adding sophisticated sound systems to C++ games improves the gamers'
overall auditory experience. In addition to introducing real-time effects,

dynamic mixing, and spatial audio, this part included demonstrations of how to incorporate FMOD Studio and OpenAL into your game.

Implementing audio in game development

Including sound in your C++ game is essential to making it immersive and interesting. Including sound effects, background music, and dynamic audio responses are just a few of the audio features that can be effectively included with the help of this area. Examples and snippets of code are provided to show how the implementation is done.

Playing Sound Effects

Sound effects add depth and feedback to in-game events. The following example demonstrates how to play a sound effect using the SFML library:

```cpp
#include <SFML/Audio.hpp>

int main() {
    // Create a sound buffer and load sound effect
    sf::SoundBuffer buffer;
    if (!buffer.loadFromFile("explosion.wav")) {
        // Handle loading error
        return -1;
    }

    // Create a sound and set its buffer
    sf::Sound sound;
    sound.setBuffer(buffer);

    // Play the sound effect
    sound.play();

    // Wait for the sound to finish (optional)
    while (sound.getStatus() == sf::Sound::Playing) {
        // Keep the program running
```

```
    }

    return 0;
}
```

Replace "explosion.wav" with the path to your sound effect file. SFML simplifies sound handling and provides features for controlling playback.

Background Music

Background music sets the tone and atmosphere of your game. The following example demonstrates how to play background music using SFML:

```cpp
#include <SFML/Audio.hpp>

int main() {
    // Create a music object and load background music
    sf::Music music;
    if (!music.openFromFile("background_music.ogg")) {
        // Handle loading error
        return -1;
    }

    // Play the background music
    music.play();

    // Keep the program running to allow background music playback
    while (true) {
        // Your game logic here
    }

    return 0;
}
```

Replace "background_music.ogg" with the path to your background music file. SFML's **Music** class provides features for controlling music playback.

Dynamic Audio Responses

Player immersion is increased when dynamic audio replies are produced in reaction to in-game events. The SFML example that follows shows how to incorporate dynamic audio responses:

```cpp
#include <SFML/Audio.hpp>

class AudioEngine {
private:
    sf::SoundBuffer buffer;
    sf::Sound sound;

public:
    AudioEngine(const std::string& soundFilePath) {
        if (!buffer.loadFromFile(soundFilePath)) {
            // Handle loading error
        }

        sound.setBuffer(buffer);
    }

    void playSound() {
        sound.play();
    }
};

int main() {
    AudioEngine audioEngine("powerup.wav");

    // Simulate in-game event
    audioEngine.playSound();

    // Keep the program running
    while (true) {
        // Your game logic here
    }

    return 0;
```

```
}
```

Replace "powerup.wav" with the path to your sound effect file. This example encapsulates audio functionality within an **AudioEngine** class for modular and organized code.

The process of incorporating sound effects, background music, and dynamic audio responses into C++ game programming is known as audio implementation. This section demonstrated how to build these audio aspects using real-world examples and the SFML library.

Audio optimization and best practices

A fluid and responsive game experience depends on effective audio implementation. The optimization methods and recommended practices for including audio in your C++ game are covered in this section. The application of various optimization algorithms is demonstrated with the help of examples and code snippets.

Streaming Large Audio Files

Streaming is a more memory-efficient method than loading the complete audio file into memory when working with huge files. The example that follows shows you how to use SFML to stream a huge background music file:

```cpp
#include <SFML/Audio.hpp>

int main() {
    sf::Music music;

    // Open the music file in streaming mode
    if (!music.openFromFile("large_music.ogg")) {
        // Handle loading error
        return -1;
```

```
    }

    // Play the streamed music
    music.play();

    // Keep the program running to allow music playback
    while (true) {
        // Your game logic here
    }

    return 0;
}
```

Replace "large_music.ogg" with the path to your large music file. Streaming allows the game to play audio without loading the entire file into memory.

Audio Compression

By reducing file size without sacrificing quality, audio compression maximizes memory and storage utilization. The usage of compressed sound effects with SFML is illustrated in the example that follows:

```
#include <SFML/Audio.hpp>

int main() {
    sf::SoundBuffer buffer;

    // Load the compressed sound effect
    if (!buffer.loadFromFile("compressed_sound.ogg")) {
        // Handle loading error
        return -1;
    }

    // Create a sound and set its buffer
    sf::Sound sound;
    sound.setBuffer(buffer);
```

```cpp
// Play the compressed sound effect
sound.play();

// Wait for the sound to finish (optional)
while (sound.getStatus() == sf::Sound::Playing) {
    // Keep the program running
}

return 0;
}
```

Replace "compressed_sound.ogg" with the path to your compressed sound effect file. Utilizing compressed audio files reduces storage requirements and speeds up loading times.

Prioritizing Audio Events

Setting audio events as priorities guarantees that important noises are heard even when processing is intensive. The example that follows shows you how to use SFML to handle and prioritize numerous audio events:

```cpp
#include <SFML/Audio.hpp>

int main() {
    sf::SoundBuffer buffer1, buffer2;

    // Load sound effects
    if (!buffer1.loadFromFile("critical_sound.wav") ||
        !buffer2.loadFromFile("background_event.wav")) {
        // Handle loading error
        return -1;
    }

    // Create sounds and set their buffers
    sf::Sound criticalSound, backgroundEvent;
    criticalSound.setBuffer(buffer1);
```

```cpp
    backgroundEvent.setBuffer(buffer2);

    // Set priorities
    criticalSound.setPriority(100); // Higher priority for
    critical sound

    // Play the sounds
    criticalSound.play();
    backgroundEvent.play();

    // Wait for the sounds to finish (optional)
    while (criticalSound.getStatus() == sf::Sound::Playing ||
    backgroundEvent.getStatus() == sf::Sound::Playing) {
        // Keep the program running
    }

    return 0;
}
```

In this example, the **setPriority** function sets a higher priority for the critical sound, ensuring it takes precedence over other sounds.

In C++ game programming, audio optimization entails streaming big files, audio compression, and sound priority. We discussed real-world examples of various optimization strategies using the SFML library. Think about how these techniques lead to a more effective and pleasurable gaming experience as you improve your game.

Implementing AI in Games

The gaming experience is made more realistic, challenging, and nuanced when Artificial Intelligence (AI) is incorporated into the game. This chapter examines a variety of AI approaches and offers real-world examples of how they are used in C++ game development.

Basic NPC Movement

One essential first step in developing AI-driven characters is to provide basic NPC mobility. The example below shows how to use SFML to construct a basic NPC class with basic movement in a 2D game:

```cpp
#include <SFML/Graphics.hpp>

class NPC {
private:
    sf::CircleShape shape;  // NPC representation
    sf::Vector2f velocity;  // NPC velocity

public:
    NPC(float radius, sf::Vector2f position, sf::Vector2f
    initialVelocity)
        : shape(radius), velocity(initialVelocity) {
        shape.setPosition(position);
    }

    void update(float deltaTime) {
```

```cpp
        // Update NPC position based on velocity
        shape.move(velocity * deltaTime);
    }

    void draw(sf::RenderWindow& window) const {
        window.draw(shape);
    }
};

int main() {
    sf::RenderWindow window(sf::VideoMode(800, 600), "Basic NPC
    Movement");

    NPC npc(20.0f, sf::Vector2f(100.0f, 100.0f),
    sf::Vector2f(50.0f, 0.0f));

    sf::Clock clock;

    while (window.isOpen()) {
        sf::Event event;
        while (window.pollEvent(event)) {
            if (event.type == sf::Event::Closed) {
                window.close();
            }
        }

        // Update NPC based on elapsed time
        float deltaTime = clock.restart().asSeconds();
        npc.update(deltaTime);

        window.clear();
        // Draw NPC
        npc.draw(window);
        window.display();
    }

    return 0;
}
```

This example creates a simple circular NPC that moves horizontally across the screen. The NPC's movement is updated based on its velocity.

Pathfinding with A* Algorithm

When pathfinding is used, game characters may intelligently traverse across challenging landscapes. An example of using the A* method for pathfinding in a two-dimensional grid-based game is provided below:

```cpp
#include <iostream>
#include <vector>
#include <queue>
#include <SFML/Graphics.hpp>

struct Node {
    int x, y;  // Node coordinates
    bool obstacle;  // Indicates whether the node is an obstacle

    // Additional fields for A* algorithm
    int g, h;  // Cost values
    Node* parent;  // Parent node

    Node(int x, int y, bool obstacle = false)
        : x(x), y(y), obstacle(obstacle), g(0), h(0),
          parent(nullptr) {}

    // Calculate the total cost (f) of the node
    int f() const {
        return g + h;
    }
};

class Pathfinding {
private:
    std::vector<std::vector<Node>> grid;  // 2D grid of nodes
    int rows, cols;  // Grid dimensions

public:
    Pathfinding(int rows, int cols)
```

```cpp
        : rows(rows), cols(cols) {
        // Initialize the grid with nodes
        grid.resize(rows, std::vector<Node>(cols));

        // Initialize nodes and set obstacles (for demonstration
        purposes)
        for (int i = 0; i < rows; ++i) {
            for (int j = 0; j < cols; ++j) {
                // Set obstacles randomly
                bool obstacle = (rand() % 100) < 20;  // 20%
                chance of obstacle
                grid[i][j] = Node(i, j, obstacle);
            }
        }
    }

    // A* algorithm for pathfinding
    std::vector<Node*> findPath(const Node& start, const Node&
    goal) {
        std::priority_queue<Node*, std::vector<Node*>,
        CompareNodes> openSet;

        // Add the start node to the open set
        openSet.push(const_cast<Node*>(&start));

        while (!openSet.empty()) {
            // Get the node with the lowest total cost (f) from
            the open set
            Node* current = openSet.top();
            openSet.pop();

            // Check if the goal is reached
            if (current == &goal) {
                return reconstructPath(&goal);
            }

            // Explore neighbors
            for (int i = -1; i <= 1; ++i) {
                for (int j = -1; j <= 1; ++j) {
                    // Skip the current node
```

```cpp
if (i == 0 && j == 0) {
    continue;
}

int neighborX = current->x + i;
int neighborY = current->y + j;

// Check if the neighbor is within the grid
bounds
if (neighborX >= 0 && neighborX < rows &&
neighborY >= 0 && neighborY < cols) {
    Node* neighbor =
    &grid[neighborX][neighborY];

    // Skip obstacles
    if (neighbor->obstacle) {
        continue;
    }

    // Calculate tentative g value
    int tentativeG = current->g + 1;

    // Check if this path to the neighbor is
    better than the current one
    if (tentativeG < neighbor->g ||
    neighbor->g == 0) {
        neighbor->g = tentativeG;
        neighbor->h = heuristic(*neighbor,
        goal);
        neighbor->parent = current;

        // Add the neighbor to the open set if
        not already present
        if (std::find(openSet.c.begin(),
        openSet.end(), neighbor) ==
        openSet.end()) {
            openSet.push(neighbor);
        }
    }
}
```

```cpp
            }
        }
    }

    // No path found
    return {};
}

// Heuristic function for A* algorithm (Euclidean distance)
int heuristic(const Node& a, const Node& b) const {
    return static_cast<int>(std::sqrt((a.x - b.x) * (a.x -
    b.x) + (a.y - b.y) * (a.y - b.y)));
}

// Compare nodes based on their total cost (f)
struct CompareNodes {
    bool operator()(const Node* a, const Node* b) const {
        return a->f() > b->f();
    }
};

// Reconstruct the path from the goal to the start
std::vector<Node*> reconstructPath(Node* goal) const {
    std::vector<Node*> path;
    Node* current = goal;

    while (current != nullptr) {
        path.push_back(current);
        current = current->parent;
    }

    std::reverse(path.begin(), path.end());
    return path;
}
};

int main() {
    // Create a window
    sf::RenderWindow window(sf::VideoMode(800, 600), "A*
    Pathfinding");
```

```cpp
// Initialize pathfinding grid
Pathfinding pathfinding(20, 20);

// Define start and goal nodes
Node start(0, 0);
Node goal(19, 19);

// Find the path using A* algorithm
std::vector<Node*> path = pathfinding.findPath(start, goal);

// Main loop
while (window.isOpen()) {
    sf::Event event;
    while (window.pollEvent(event)) {
        if (event.type == sf::Event::Closed) {
            window.close();
        }
    }

    window.clear();

    // Draw the grid
    for (int i = 0; i < pathfinding.getRows(); ++i) {
        for (int j = 0; j < pathfinding.getCols(); ++j) {
            sf::RectangleShape rect(sf::Vector2f(30.0f,
            30.0f));
            rect.setPosition(j * 30.0f, i * 30.0f);

            // Color obstacles in red
            if (pathfinding.getNode(i, j).obstacle) {
                rect.setFillColor(sf::Color::Red);
            } else {
                rect.setFillColor(sf::Color::White);
            }

            window.draw(rect);
        }
    }
```

```cpp
            // Draw the path
            for (const Node* node : path) {
                sf::RectangleShape rect(sf::Vector2f(30.0f, 30.0f));
                rect.setPosition(node->y * 30.0f, node->x * 30.0f);
                rect.setFillColor(sf::Color::Green);
                window.draw(rect);
            }

            window.display();
        }

        // Cleanup allocated memory for the path
        for (Node* node : path) {
            delete node;
        }

        return 0;
    }
```

This example demonstrates a simple 2D grid-based game where an NPC (represented by a green circle) navigates through obstacles (red squares) using the A* algorithm for pathfinding. The A* algorithm efficiently calculates the shortest path from the NPC's starting position to the goal.

Intelligent, engaging, and difficult gaming experiences may be made in a myriad of ways by integrating AI into C++ game programming. Basic NPC movement and sophisticated pathfinding with the A* algorithm were covered in this part.

AI techniques and algorithms

The behavior of game characters is greatly influenced by AI methods and algorithms, which results in vibrant and captivating gaming experiences. The Behavior Trees algorithm and finite state machines will be discussed in this part.

Finite State Machines (FSM)

An agent's behavior is modeled by finite state machines, a basic idea in artificial intelligence, as a collection of states, transitions, and actions. An example of a basic implementation of a simple NPC using an FSM is shown below:

```cpp
#include <iostream>

// Define possible states
enum class State { Idle, Patrol, Chase };

class NPC {
private:
    State currentState;

public:
    NPC() : currentState(State::Idle) {}

    // Update NPC behavior based on the current state
    void update() {
        switch (currentState) {
            case State::Idle:
                std::cout << "NPC is idling.\n";
                // Transition to Patrol or Chase based on certain
                conditions
                break;

            case State::Patrol:
                std::cout << "NPC is patrolling.\n";
                // Transition to Idle or Chase based on certain
                conditions
                break;

            case State::Chase:
                std::cout << "NPC is chasing the player.\n";
                // Transition to Idle or Patrol based on certain
                conditions
                break;
```

```cpp
        }
    }

    // Set the NPC's current state
    void setState(State newState) {
        currentState = newState;
    }
};

int main() {
    NPC npc;

    // Simulate game loop
    for (int i = 0; i < 5; ++i) {
        npc.update();
        // Perform other game-related tasks
    }

    return 0;
}
```

In this example, the NPC's behavior is represented by three states: Idle, Patrol, and Chase. The NPC transitions between states based on certain conditions, creating dynamic behavior.

Behavior Trees

Behavior Trees provide a hierarchical way to structure AI behavior. The following example demonstrates a basic implementation of a behavior tree for an NPC:

```cpp
#include <iostream>

// Define possible actions
enum class Action { MoveTo, Attack, Idle };

// Define the Behavior Tree node
```

```cpp
class BehaviorNode {
public:
    virtual Action evaluate() = 0;
};

// Composite node: Sequence
class SequenceNode : public BehaviorNode {
private:
    BehaviorNode* left;
    BehaviorNode* right;

public:
    SequenceNode(BehaviorNode* left, BehaviorNode* right) :
    left(left), right(right) {}

    Action evaluate() override {
        // Evaluate left child
        Action result = left->evaluate();

        // If successful, evaluate right child
        if (result != Action::Idle) {
            result = right->evaluate();
        }

        return result;
    }
};

// Leaf node: MoveTo
class MoveToNode : public BehaviorNode {
public:
    Action evaluate() override {
        std::cout << "NPC is moving to a location.\n";
        // Perform actual movement logic
        return Action::MoveTo;
    }
};

// Leaf node: Attack
class AttackNode : public BehaviorNode {
```

```cpp
public:
    Action evaluate() override {
        std::cout << "NPC is attacking.\n";
        // Perform actual attack logic
        return Action::Attack;
    }
};

// Leaf node: Idle
class IdleNode : public BehaviorNode {
public:
    Action evaluate() override {
        std::cout << "NPC is idling.\n";
        // Perform actual idle logic
        return Action::Idle;
    }
};

int main() {
    // Create a behavior tree for an NPC
    BehaviorNode* behaviorTree = new SequenceNode(new
    MoveToNode(), new AttackNode());

    // Simulate game loop
    for (int i = 0; i < 5; ++i) {
        Action result = behaviorTree->evaluate();
        // Perform other game-related tasks based on the result
    }

    // Cleanup allocated memory for the behavior tree
    delete behaviorTree;

    return 0;
}
```

In this example, the behavior tree consists of three types of nodes: Sequence, MoveTo, Attack, and Idle. The Sequence node evaluates its children in sequence, and if the left child succeeds, it evaluates the right child.

Integrating AI into gameplay

The intricacy and depth of gaming worlds are increased when AI is incorporated into gameplay. Reactive AI for dynamic interactions, decision-making
via behavior trees, and dynamic NPC behavior utilizing finite state machines
are all covered in this area.

Creating engrossing and difficult gaming experiences requires incorporating
Artificial Intelligence (AI) into the gameplay. We will examine real-world
applications of AI integration in C++ game development, including dynamic
interactions, decision-making, and NPC behavior.

Dynamic NPC Behavior Using Finite State Machines (FSM)

A useful technique for simulating NPC behavior is a finite state machine. We'll
construct an NPC class in this example that dynamically switches between
several states using an FSM:

```cpp
#include <iostream>
#include <ctime>

// Define possible states
enum class State { Idle, Patrol, Chase };

class NPC {
private:
    State currentState;

public:
    NPC() : currentState(State::Idle) {}

    // Update NPC behavior based on the current state
    void update() {
        switch (currentState) {
```

```cpp
        case State::Idle:
            std::cout << "NPC is idling.\n";
            // Transition to Patrol or Chase based on certain
            conditions
            if (rand() % 100 < 20) {
                currentState = State::Patrol;
            } else if (rand() % 100 < 30) {
                currentState = State::Chase;
            }
            break;

        case State::Patrol:
            std::cout << "NPC is patrolling.\n";
            // Transition to Idle or Chase based on certain
            conditions
            if (rand() % 100 < 20) {
                currentState = State::Idle;
            } else if (rand() % 100 < 30) {
                currentState = State::Chase;
            }
            break;

        case State::Chase:
            std::cout << "NPC is chasing the player.\n";
            // Transition to Idle or Patrol based on certain
            conditions
            if (rand() % 100 < 20) {
                currentState = State::Idle;
            } else if (rand() % 100 < 30) {
                currentState = State::Patrol;
            }
            break;
        }
    }
};

int main() {
    // Seed for random number generation
    std::srand(static_cast<unsigned>(std::time(nullptr)));
```

```
    NPC npc;

    // Simulate game loop
    for (int i = 0; i < 5; ++i) {
        npc.update();
        // Perform other game-related tasks
    }

    return 0;
}
```

In this example, the NPC class updates its behavior in the game loop based on the current state. Transitions between states are triggered by certain conditions, creating dynamic and responsive NPC behavior.

Decision-Making with Behavior Trees

Behavior Trees give gaming characters a hierarchical framework for making decisions. We'll construct an NPC class in this example, and it will use a Behavior Tree to make decisions:

```cpp
#include <iostream>

// Define possible actions
enum class Action { MoveTo, Attack, Idle };

// Define the Behavior Tree node
class BehaviorNode {
public:
    virtual Action evaluate() = 0;
};

// Composite node: Sequence
class SequenceNode : public BehaviorNode {
private:
    BehaviorNode* left;
```

```cpp
    BehaviorNode* right;

public:
    SequenceNode(BehaviorNode* left, BehaviorNode* right) :
    left(left), right(right) {}

    Action evaluate() override {
        // Evaluate left child
        Action result = left->evaluate();

        // If successful, evaluate right child
        if (result != Action::Idle) {
            result = right->evaluate();
        }

        return result;
    }
};

// Leaf node: MoveTo
class MoveToNode : public BehaviorNode {
public:
    Action evaluate() override {
        std::cout << "NPC is moving to a location.\n";
        // Perform actual movement logic
        return Action::MoveTo;
    }
};

// Leaf node: Attack
class AttackNode : public BehaviorNode {
public:
    Action evaluate() override {
        std::cout << "NPC is attacking.\n";
        // Perform actual attack logic
        return Action::Attack;
    }
};

// Leaf node: Idle
```

```cpp
class IdleNode : public BehaviorNode {
public:
    Action evaluate() override {
        std::cout << "NPC is idling.\n";
        // Perform actual idle logic
        return Action::Idle;
    }
};


class NPC {
private:
    BehaviorNode* behaviorTree;

public:
    NPC() {
        // Create a behavior tree for the NPC
        behaviorTree = new SequenceNode(new MoveToNode(), new
        AttackNode());
    }

    // Update NPC behavior based on the behavior tree
    void update() {
        Action result = behaviorTree->evaluate();
        // Perform other game-related tasks based on the result
    }

    // Cleanup allocated memory for the behavior tree
    ~NPC() {
        delete behaviorTree;
    }
};

int main() {
    NPC npc;

    // Simulate game loop
    for (int i = 0; i < 5; ++i) {
        npc.update();
        // Perform other game-related tasks
    }
```

```
    return 0;
}
```

In this example, the NPC class uses a Behavior Tree to make decisions. The Behavior Tree consists of nodes representing actions (e.g., MoveTo, Attack, Idle) and a Sequence node to evaluate actions in a specific order.

Reactive AI for Dynamic Interactions

NPCs can react dynamically to player actions and the game environment thanks to reactive AI. We'll develop an NPC class in this example that reacts to player proximity:

```cpp
#include <iostream>

class Player {
public:
    void onApproach() {
        std::cout << "Player is approaching.\n";
        // Perform actions when the player approaches
    }
};

class NPC {
private:
    Player* player;

public:
    NPC(Player* player) : player(player) {}

    // Update NPC behavior based on player proximity
    void update() {
        // Check player proximity (for demonstration purposes)
        if (rand() % 100 < 30) {
            player->onApproach();
        }
```

```cpp
        // Perform other game-related tasks
    }
};

int main() {
    // Seed for random number generation
    std::srand(static_cast<unsigned>(std::time(nullptr)));

    Player player;
    NPC npc(&player);

    // Simulate game loop
    for (int i = 0; i < 5; ++i) {
        npc.update();
        // Perform other game-related tasks
    }

    return 0;
}
```

In this example, the NPC class checks for player proximity during the game
loop. If the player is approaching (determined by a random condition), the
NPC reacts by calling the **onApproach** function of the Player class.

Creating intelligent and challenging opponents

One of the most important aspects of game development that greatly enhances
the player experience is the creation of clever and difficult opponents. This
section covers C++ game programming strategies for creating opponents with
complex behavior, decision-making, and adaptability.

Adaptive AI with Decision Trees

Decision trees are excellent resources for modeling adversaries' adaptive
behavior. Here, we'll put in place a simple decision tree for an adversary
that modifies its approach in response to the player's actions:

```cpp
#include <iostream>

// Define possible actions
enum class Action { Attack, Defend, Retreat };

// Define the Decision Tree node
class DecisionNode {
public:
    virtual Action evaluate() = 0;
};

// Composite node: Sequence
class SequenceNode : public DecisionNode {
private:
    DecisionNode* left;
    DecisionNode* right;

public:
    SequenceNode(DecisionNode* left, DecisionNode* right) :
    left(left), right(right) {}

    Action evaluate() override {
        // Evaluate left child
        Action result = left->evaluate();

        // If successful, evaluate right child
        if (result != Action::Retreat) {
            result = right->evaluate();
        }

        return result;
    }
};

// Leaf node: Attack
class AttackNode : public DecisionNode {
public:
    Action evaluate() override {
```

```cpp
        std::cout << "Opponent is attacking.\n";
        // Perform actual attack logic
        return Action::Attack;
    }
};

// Leaf node: Defend
class DefendNode : public DecisionNode {
public:
    Action evaluate() override {
        std::cout << "Opponent is defending.\n";
        // Perform actual defend logic
        return Action::Defend;
    }
};

// Leaf node: Retreat
class RetreatNode : public DecisionNode {
public:
    Action evaluate() override {
        std::cout << "Opponent is retreating.\n";
        // Perform actual retreat logic
        return Action::Retreat;
    }
};

class Opponent {
private:
    DecisionNode* decisionTree;

public:
    Opponent() {
        // Create a decision tree for the opponent
        decisionTree = new SequenceNode(new AttackNode(), new
        DefendNode());
    }

    // Update opponent behavior based on the decision tree
    void update() {
        Action result = decisionTree->evaluate();
```

```cpp
        // Perform other game-related tasks based on the result
    }

    // Cleanup allocated memory for the decision tree
    ~Opponent() {
        delete decisionTree;
    }
};

int main() {
    Opponent opponent;

    // Simulate game loop
    for (int i = 0; i < 5; ++i) {
        opponent.update();
        // Perform other game-related tasks
    }

    return 0;
}
```

In this example, the opponent class uses a Decision Tree to determine its actions. The Decision Tree consists of nodes representing actions (e.g., Attack, Defend, Retreat) and a Sequence node to evaluate actions in a specific order.

Learning AI with Reinforcement Learning

Reinforcement Learning allows opponents to adapt and learn from their experiences. In this example, we'll implement a basic reinforcement learning algorithm for an opponent:

```cpp
#include <iostream>

// Define possible actions
enum class Action { Attack, Defend, Retreat };

class Opponent {
```

```cpp
private:
    // Q-values representing the expected rewards for each action
    float qValues[3] = {0.0f, 0.0f, 0.0f};
    float learningRate = 0.1f;  // Learning rate
    float discountFactor = 0.9f;  // Discount factor for future
    rewards

public:
    // Select an action based on the current Q-values
    Action selectAction() {
        // Explore or exploit strategy (for demonstration purposes)
        if (rand() % 100 < 20) {
            return static_cast<Action>(rand() % 3);
        } else {
            // Exploit: Select the action with the highest Q-value
            int maxIndex = 0;
            for (int i = 1; i < 3; ++i) {
                if (qValues[i] > qValues[maxIndex]) {
                    maxIndex = i;
                }
            }
            return static_cast<Action>(maxIndex);
        }
    }

    // Update Q-values based on the observed reward
    void updateQValues(Action selectedAction, float reward) {
        // Update Q-value for the selected action using the
        Bellman equation
        qValues[static_cast<int>(selectedAction)] +=
            learningRate * (reward + discountFactor *
            getMaxQValue() -
            qValues[static_cast<int>(selectedAction)]);
    }

    // Get the Q-value for the action with the highest Q-value
    float getMaxQValue() const {
        float maxQValue = qValues[0];
        for (int i = 1; i < 3; ++i) {
            if (qValues[i] > maxQValue) {
```

```cpp
                    maxQValue = qValues[i];
            }
        }
        return maxQValue;
    }

    // Simulate opponent's action and receive a reward
    void simulateAction() {
        // For demonstration purposes, simulate receiving a reward
        float reward = static_cast<float>(rand() % 100) / 100.0f;
        std::cout << "Received reward: " << reward << "\n";

        // Select an action based on the current Q-values
        Action selectedAction = selectAction();

        // Update Q-values based on the observed reward
        updateQValues(selectedAction, reward);

        // Perform other game-related tasks based on the selected
        action and reward
        // ...
    }
};

int main() {
    // Seed for random number generation
    std::srand(static_cast<unsigned>(std::time(nullptr)));

    Opponent opponent;

    // Simulate multiple iterations of the learning process
    for (int i = 0; i < 5; ++i) {
        opponent.simulateAction();
    }

    return 0;
}
```

In this example, the opponent class uses a basic reinforcement learning algorithm to adapt its strategy based on the observed rewards. The Q-values represent the expected rewards for each action, and the opponent learns by updating these values over time.

Responsive AI with Finite State Machines

It is possible to create opponents with responsive behavior by extending Finite State Machines. We'll create an opponent class in this example that dynamically switches between several states using an FSM:

```cpp
#include <iostream>
#include <ctime>

// Define possible states
enum class State { Idle, Attack, Defend, Retreat };

class Opponent {
private:
    State currentState;

public:
    Opponent() : currentState(State::Idle) {}

    // Update opponent behavior based on the current state
    void update() {
        switch (currentState) {
            case State::Idle:
                std::cout << "Opponent is idling.\n";
                // Transition to Attack, Defend, or Retreat based
                on certain conditions
                if (rand() % 100 < 30) {
                    currentState = State::Attack;
                } else if (rand() % 100 < 20) {
                    currentState = State::Defend;
                } else if (rand() % 100 < 10) {
                    currentState = State::Retreat;
                }
                break;
```

```cpp
            case State::Attack:
                std::cout << "Opponent is attacking.\n";
                // Transition to Idle or Defend based on certain
                conditions
                if (rand() % 100 < 40) {
                    currentState = State::Idle;
                } else if (rand() % 100 < 20) {
                    currentState = State::Defend;
                }
                break;

            case State::Defend:
                std::cout << "Opponent is defending.\n";
                // Transition to Idle or Attack based on certain
                conditions
                if (rand() % 100 < 40) {
                    currentState = State::Idle;
                } else if (rand() % 100 < 20) {
                    currentState = State::Attack;
                }
                break;

            case State::Retreat:
                std::cout << "Opponent is retreating.\n";
                // Transition to Idle based on certain conditions
                if (rand() % 100 < 30) {
                    currentState = State::Idle;
                }
                break;
        }
    }
};

int main() {
    // Seed for random number generation
    std::srand(static_cast<unsigned>(std::time(nullptr)));

    Opponent opponent;

    // Simulate game loop
```

```
    for (int i = 0; i < 5; ++i) {
        opponent.update();
        // Perform other game-related tasks
    }

    return 0;
}
```

In this example, the opponent class uses an FSM to dynamically switch between states, representing different behaviors. Transitions between states are triggered by certain conditions, creating opponents with responsive and adaptive behavior.

Developing smart and difficult adversaries is a complex task that combines responsive behavior, learning mechanisms, and decision-making algorithms. We've discussed how to create AI opponents who are responsive with finite state machines, learn AI through reinforcement learning, and use decision trees for adaptive AI design. In order to create a compelling player experience, balance the degree of difficulty and take into account the unique demands of your game design as you implement these strategies into your C++ game development. Into the next section.

****

Networking and Multiplayer Games

Networking Essentials for Multiplayer Games

In multiplayer games, users can communicate with one another in a shared virtual environment using networking. The fundamental ideas and methods for integrating networking into C++ game development are examined in this chapter, which covers subjects including synchronization, communication protocols, and client-server architecture.

Client-Server Architecture

A typical design in multiplayer games is the client-server architecture, in which several machines (clients) connect to the server to play, while one system (the server) holds the game logic and state. This is a simple example of a C++ server and client implementation that makes use of sockets:

Server (simplified):

```cpp
#include <iostream>
#include <WS2tcpip.h>
#pragma comment(lib, "ws2_32.lib")

int main() {
    // Initialize Winsock
    WSADATA wsData;
    WORD ver = MAKEWORD(2, 2);
```

```cpp
int wsOk = WSAStartup(ver, &wsData);
if (wsOk != 0) {
    std::cerr << "Can't initialize Winsock! Quitting" <<
    std::endl;
    return -1;
}

// Create a socket
SOCKET listening = socket(AF_INET, SOCK_STREAM, 0);
if (listening == INVALID_SOCKET) {
    std::cerr << "Can't create a socket! Quitting" <<
    std::endl;
    return -1;
}

// Bind the socket to an IP address and port
sockaddr_in hint;
hint.sin_family = AF_INET;
hint.sin_port = htons(54000);
hint.sin_addr.S_un.S_addr = INADDR_ANY;  // Use any address

bind(listening, (sockaddr*)&hint, sizeof(hint));

// Tell Winsock the socket is for listening
listen(listening, SOMAXCONN);

// Wait for a connection
sockaddr_in client;
int clientSize = sizeof(client);

SOCKET clientSocket = accept(listening, (sockaddr*)&client,
&clientSize);

// Close listening socket
closesocket(listening);

// While loop: accept and echo message back to client
char buf[4096];
while (true) {
    ZeroMemory(buf, 4096);
```

```cpp
        // Wait for client to send data
        int bytesReceived = recv(clientSocket, buf, 4096, 0);
        if (bytesReceived == SOCKET_ERROR) {
            std::cerr << "Error in recv. Quitting" << std::endl;
            break;
        }

        if (bytesReceived == 0) {
            std::cout << "Client disconnected" << std::endl;
            break;
        }

        std::cout << "Received: " << std::string(buf, 0,
        bytesReceived) << std::endl;

        // Echo message back to client
        send(clientSocket, buf, bytesReceived + 1, 0);
    }

    // Close the socket
    closesocket(clientSocket);

    // Cleanup Winsock
    WSACleanup();

    return 0;
}
```

Client (simplified):

```cpp
#include <iostream>
#include <WS2tcpip.h>
#pragma comment(lib, "ws2_32.lib")

int main() {
    // Initialize Winsock
    WSADATA wsData;
```

```cpp
WORD ver = MAKEWORD(2, 2);
int wsOk = WSAStartup(ver, &wsData);
if (wsOk != 0) {
    std::cerr << "Can't initialize Winsock! Quitting" <<
    std::endl;
    return -1;
}

// Create a socket
SOCKET clientSocket = socket(AF_INET, SOCK_STREAM, 0);
if (clientSocket == INVALID_SOCKET) {
    std::cerr << "Can't create a socket! Quitting" <<
    std::endl;
    return -1;
}

// Fill in the hint structure
sockaddr_in hint;
hint.sin_family = AF_INET;
hint.sin_port = htons(54000);
inet_pton(AF_INET, "127.0.0.1", &hint.sin_addr);

// Connect to the server
int connResult = connect(clientSocket, (sockaddr*)&hint,
sizeof(hint));
if (connResult == SOCKET_ERROR) {
    std::cerr << "Can't connect to server! Quitting" <<
    std::endl;
    closesocket(clientSocket);
    WSACleanup();
    return -1;
}

// Do-while loop to send and receive data
char buf[4096];
std::string userInput;

do {
    // Prompt the user for some text
    std::cout << "> ";
```

```cpp
        getline(std::cin, userInput);

        // Send the text
        if (userInput.size() > 0) {
            int sendResult = send(clientSocket, userInput.c_str(),
            userInput.size() + 1, 0);
            if (sendResult != SOCKET_ERROR) {
                // Wait for response
                ZeroMemory(buf, 4096);
                int bytesReceived = recv(clientSocket, buf, 4096,
                0);
                if (bytesReceived > 0) {
                    // Echo response to console
                    std::cout << "SERVER> " << std::string(buf, 0,
                    bytesReceived) << std::endl;
                }
            }
        }

    } while (userInput.size() > 0);

    // Close down everything
    closesocket(clientSocket);
    WSACleanup();

    return 0;
}
```

In this example, the server waits for a connection, and the client connects to the server. The server echoes back any message it receives from the client.

Communication Protocols

In order to communicate information, a specific protocol must be used during client-server communication. For your game, think about implementing a basic protocol, like transmitting messages in a predetermined format. Observe this simple example:

```cpp
// Message structure
struct Message {
    int messageType;
    // Add other relevant fields
};

// Serialize message to a char array
char* serializeMessage(const Message& message) {
    char* data = new char[sizeof(Message)];
    memcpy(data, &message, sizeof(Message));
    return data;
}

// Deserialize char array to a message
Message deserializeMessage(const char* data) {
    Message message;
    memcpy(&message, data, sizeof(Message));
    return message;
}
```

This example defines a simple message structure and provides functions to serialize and deserialize messages. Ensure that your protocol covers the necessary information for your game, such as player actions, positions, and events.

Synchronization and Game State

A reliable multiplayer experience depends on the server and clients synchronizing the game state. Here is a condensed illustration of state synchronization:

Server (partial):

```cpp
// Game state structure
struct GameState {
    // Add relevant game state fields
};
```

```cpp
// Function to send game state to a client
void sendGameState(const GameState& gameState, SOCKET
clientSocket) {
    char* data = serializeMessage({1});   // Assume message type 1
    is for game state
    send(clientSocket, data, sizeof(Message), 0);
    send(clientSocket, serializeMessage(gameState),
    sizeof(GameState), 0);
    delete[] data;
}
```

Client (partial):

```cpp
// Function to receive game state from the server
void receiveGameState(SOCKET serverSocket, GameState& gameState) {
    char* data = new char[sizeof(Message)];
    recv(serverSocket, data, sizeof(Message), 0);

    Message message = deserializeMessage(data);
    delete[] data;

    if (message.messageType == 1) {   // Assume message type 1 is
    for game state
        data = new char[sizeof(GameState)];
        recv(serverSocket, data, sizeof(GameState), 0);
        gameState = deserializeMessage(data);
        delete[] data;
    }
}
```

In this example, the server sends the game state to clients, and clients receive and update their local game state accordingly.

A thorough understanding of client-server architecture, communication protocols, and game state synchronization is necessary to implement networking in C++ game development. This section explained the significance of synchronizing game state between the server and clients, established a basic message communication protocol, and included a basic example of a client-server setup utilizing sockets. To create a smooth and entertaining multiplayer experience, take scalability, security, and optimization into consideration when you construct a multiplayer game.

Network architectures for games

Multiplayer games require a strong network architecture to be successful. This section examines many network architectures, such as peer-to-peer and client-server models, that are frequently utilized in C++ game development. It also offers implementation concerns and examples for various architectures.

Peer-to-Peer Network Architecture

Every player in the game has the ability to function as both a client and a server thanks to the peer-to-peer network architecture. Peers exchange information and game state directly with one another. Peer-to-peer architectures might be appropriate for some game kinds, but they might also pose synchronization and security issues.

Example: Basic Peer-to-Peer Connection

```
// Basic peer-to-peer connection example using sockets

// Assume the existence of functions like sendToPeer and
receiveFromPeer

class Peer {
public:
    // Function to send game state to a peer
    void sendGameState(const GameState& gameState, const Peer&
    peer) {
        sendToPeer(serializeMessage({1}), peer);
```

```
        sendToPeer(serializeMessage(gameState), peer);
    }

    // Function to receive game state from a peer
    void receiveGameState(GameState& gameState, const Peer& peer) {
        Message message =
        deserializeMessage(receiveFromPeer(peer));
        if (message.messageType == 1) {   // Assume message type 1
        is for game state
            gameState = deserializeMessage(receiveFromPeer(peer));
        }
    }
};
```

In this example, peers exchange game state directly. However, keep in mind that peer-to-peer architectures might face challenges in scenarios with a large number of participants or when strict synchronization is required.

Client-Server Network Architecture

A central server controls client-to-client communication and the game's state in the client-server network architecture. The server, which serves as a reliable source of information, is accessed by clients. This architecture can support more participants and offers more control over synchronization.

Example: Basic Client-Server Connection

Server (partial):

```
// Basic client-server connection example using sockets

// Assume the existence of functions like sendToClient and
receiveFromClient

class Server {
```

```cpp
public:
    // Function to send game state to a client
    void sendGameState(const GameState& gameState, const Client&
    client) {
        sendToClient(serializeMessage({1}), client);
        sendToClient(serializeMessage(gameState), client);
    }

    // Function to receive game state from a client
    void receiveGameState(GameState& gameState, const Client&
    client) {
        Message message =
        deserializeMessage(receiveFromClient(client));
        if (message.messageType == 1) {  // Assume message type 1
        is for game state
            gameState =
            deserializeMessage(receiveFromClient(client));
        }
    }
};
```

Client (partial):

```cpp
// Basic client-server connection example using sockets

// Assume the existence of functions like sendToServer and
receiveFromServer

class Client {
public:
    // Function to send user input to the server
    void sendUserInput(const UserInput& userInput, const Server&
    server) {
        sendToServer(serializeMessage({2}), server);
        sendToServer(serializeMessage(userInput), server);
    }

    // Function to receive game state from the server
    void receiveGameState(GameState& gameState, const Server&
```

```
server) {
    Message message =
    deserializeMessage(receiveFromServer(server));
    if (message.messageType == 1) {  // Assume message type 1
    is for game state
        gameState =
        deserializeMessage(receiveFromServer(server));
    }
  }
};
```

In this example, clients send user input to the server, and the server broadcasts the game state to all connected clients. The server acts as an authoritative source, helping to maintain a consistent game state.

Considerations and Best Practices

- **Security**: Implement secure communication protocols to prevent unauthorized access and protect sensitive data.
- **Scalability**: Design the architecture to handle a growing number of participants and minimize latency.
- **Synchronization**: Ensure that game state is synchronized accurately between participants to maintain a consistent experience.
- **Reliability**: Implement error handling and recovery mechanisms to address potential network issues.
- **Load Balancing**: For large-scale games, consider load balancing strategies to distribute player connections across multiple servers.

In C++ game development, choosing the appropriate network architecture is essential since it affects a multiplayer game's performance, scalability, and overall experience. Peer-to-peer and client-server architectures were the two popular ones covered in this section, along with implementation considerations and examples. Consider the particular needs and limitations of your project carefully when you create the network architecture for your game.

Implementing multiplayer features in C++

With multiplayer capabilities, players may interact with one another in shared virtual worlds, giving games a dynamic and captivating new dimension. In this section, we'll look at how multiplayer elements are implemented in C++ games, including real-time communication, networked entities, and player synchronization.

Player Synchronization

For a multiplayer game to be consistent and fair, it is essential that every player sees the same game state. The process of broadcasting and updating each player's position and activities over the network is known as player synchronization.

Example: Basic Player Synchronization

```cpp
// Assume the existence of a Player class with relevant attributes
and methods

// Server-side code
class Server {
public:
    // Function to broadcast player positions to all connected
    clients
    void broadcastPlayerPositions(const std::vector<Player>&
    players) {
        for (const auto& player : players) {
            // Serialize player data and send it to all clients
            sendToAllClients(serializePlayer(player));
        }
    }
```

```cpp
};

// Client-side code
class Client {
public:
    // Function to receive player positions from the server
    void receivePlayerPositions(std::vector<Player>& players) {
        // Receive serialized player data from the server
        std::string serializedData = receiveFromServer();

        // Deserialize and update player positions
        Player player = deserializePlayer(serializedData);
        updatePlayerPosition(player);
    }
};
```

In this example, the server broadcasts player positions to all connected clients, and each client receives and updates the positions accordingly. Serialization and deserialization functions are assumed to be implemented for transmitting player data over the network.

Networked Entities

Networked entities can be any object, enemy, or interactive element found in the game world, in addition to player synchronization. A cooperative and engaging multiplayer experience is enhanced by the network's ability to transmit and update the state of these entities.

Example: Basic Networked Entity Synchronization

```cpp
// Assume the existence of a NetworkedEntity class with relevant
attributes and methods

// Server-side code
class Server {
public:
```

```cpp
    // Function to broadcast networked entity positions to all
    connected clients
    void broadcastEntityPositions(const
    std::vector<NetworkedEntity>& entities) {
        for (const auto& entity : entities) {
            // Serialize entity data and send it to all clients
            sendToAllClients(serializeEntity(entity));
        }
    }
};


// Client-side code
class Client {
public:
    // Function to receive networked entity positions from the
    server
    void receiveEntityPositions(std::vector<NetworkedEntity>&
    entities) {
        // Receive serialized entity data from the server
        std::string serializedData = receiveFromServer();

        // Deserialize and update entity positions
        NetworkedEntity entity = deserializeEntity(serializedData);
        updateEntityPosition(entity);
    }
};
```

This example mirrors the player synchronization approach but extends it to handle networked entities. Each client receives and updates the positions of these entities to maintain a consistent game state.

Real-Time Communication

For multiplayer to function smoothly, real-time communication is essential. The responsiveness and interactivity of the game are improved by putting in place systems for effectively transmitting data in real time between clients and the server.

Example: Real-Time Communication with Sockets

```cpp
// Server-side code
class Server {
public:
    // Function to handle real-time communication with clients
    void handleRealTimeCommunication() {
        while (true) {
            // Receive real-time input or actions from a client
            std::string input = receiveFromClient();

            // Process input and update the game state

            // Broadcast the updated game state to all clients
            broadcastUpdatedGameState();
        }
    }
};


// Client-side code
class Client {
public:
    // Function to send real-time input or actions to the server
    void sendRealTimeInput(const std::string& input) {
        sendToServer(input);
    }

    // Function to receive the updated game state in real-time
    void receiveUpdatedGameState() {
        // Receive serialized game state data from the server
        std::string serializedData = receiveFromServer();

        // Deserialize and update the local game state
        GameState gameState = deserializeGameState(serializedData);
        updateLocalGameState(gameState);
    }
};
```

In this example, the server continuously receives real-time input or actions
from clients, processes the input to update the game state, and then broadcasts

the updated game state to all connected clients. Clients send their real-time input to the server and receive the updated game state in return.

In C++ game development, real-time communication, networked entity management, and player synchronization are needed to implement multiplayer features. Examples of simple synchronization techniques for players and networked entities were given in this part, along with a socket-based real-time communication architecture. Scalability, security, and optimization should all be taken into account when adding multiplayer capabilities to your game in order to guarantee a smooth multiplayer experience.

Handling synchronization and latency issues

When creating a multiplayer game, synchronization and latency are essential components. This section will provide methods for addressing synchronization issues and reducing latency in C++ game development. Lag compensation, server reconciliation, and client-side prediction are among the subjects covered.

Client-Side Prediction

By enabling clients to anticipate their state changes without waiting for confirmation from the server, client-side prediction improves the responsiveness of player activities. Corrections can be made when server updates occur, even though projections might not always match the authoritative state of the server.

Example: Basic Client-Side Prediction

```
// Assume the existence of a Player class with relevant attributes
and methods
```

```cpp
// Client-side code
class Client {
private:
    Player localPlayer;
    std::vector<Player> remotePlayers;

public:
    // Function to predict the local player's movement
    void predictLocalPlayerMovement(float deltaTime) {
        localPlayer.predictMovement(deltaTime);
    }

    // Function to apply corrections based on server updates
    void applyServerCorrections(const Player& correctedPlayer) {
        localPlayer.correctPosition(correctedPlayer.getPosition());
    }

    // Function to update remote player positions
    void updateRemotePlayerPositions(const std::vector<Player>&
    updatedPlayers) {
        remotePlayers = updatedPlayers;
    }
};
```

In this example, the local player predicts their movement based on user input, and corrections are applied when the server sends authoritative updates. Remote player positions are updated based on information received from the server.

Server Reconciliation

A method to resolve inconsistent state updates between the client and server is server reconciliation. Adjustments are made to get the client back in sync when its anticipated state differs from the server's authoritative state.

Example: Basic Server Reconciliation

```cpp
// Assume the existence of a Player class with relevant attributes
and methods

// Server-side code
class Server {
private:
    std::unordered_map<int, Player> players; // PlayerID -> Player

public:
    // Function to reconcile client predictions with authoritative
    server state
    void reconcileClientPrediction(int clientID, const Player&
    clientPrediction) {
        Player& authoritativeState = players[clientID];

        // Compare client prediction with authoritative state
        if (!isPredictionCorrect(clientPrediction,
        authoritativeState)) {
            // Apply corrections to bring the client in sync
            sendCorrectionToClient(clientID, authoritativeState);
        }
    }
};
```

In this example, the server reconciles the client's predicted state with the authoritative state. If discrepancies are detected, corrections are sent to the client to ensure synchronization.

Lag Compensation

By accounting for the time lag that occurs between a client's action and the server's acknowledgment, lag compensation mitigates the problems caused by network latency. This guarantees that every player, irrespective of their network conditions, perceives actions in an identical manner.

Example: Basic Lag Compensation

```cpp
// Assume the existence of a Player class with relevant attributes
and methods

// Server-side code
class Server {
public:
    // Function to compensate for network lag and provide
    acknowledgment
    void processClientAction(int clientID, const PlayerAction&
    action) {
        // Simulate network latency
        simulateNetworkLatency();

        // Process the client's action and update the game state
        updateGameState(action);

        // Send acknowledgment with compensated timestamp to the
        client
        sendAcknowledgmentToClient(clientID,
        compensateForLatency(action.getTimestamp()));
    }
};
```

In this example, the server compensates for network latency when processing client actions. Acknowledgments sent to clients include a compensated timestamp, allowing them to align their predictions with the server's authoritative state.

Managing latency and synchronization problems is crucial to providing a fluid multiplayer gaming experience. To solve these issues, this section proposed methods like latency compensation, server reconciliation, and client-side prediction. When using these tactics to your C++ game, keep in mind the particular needs of the project and strive for a balance between accuracy and responsiveness.

Advanced Topics and Optimization

Cross-Platform Development

Making games playable across a variety of platforms and operating systems is essential for expanding the game's audience. This chapter will discuss methods and resources for C++ game programming that enable cross-platform interoperability.

Using Cross-Platform Libraries

The development process can be streamlined by using cross-platform libraries, which offer a single API that abstracts platform-specific aspects. Graphics Library Framework (GLFW) and SDL (Simple DirectMedia Layer) are two well-liked cross-platform libraries for game development.

Example: Cross-Platform Input Handling with SDL

```cpp
#include <SDL.h>

// Cross-platform input handling using SDL
class InputHandler {
public:
    // Initialize SDL and set up input
    bool initialize() {
        if (SDL_Init(SDL_INIT_VIDEO) < 0) {
            // Handle initialization error
            return false;
        }
```

```cpp
        // Additional initialization code

        return true;
    }

    // Handle input events
    void handleInput() {
        SDL_Event event;
        while (SDL_PollEvent(&event) != 0) {
            if (event.type == SDL_QUIT) {
                // Handle quit event
            }
            // Additional event handling
        }
    }

    // Clean up resources
    void cleanup() {
        SDL_Quit();
    }
};
```

In this example, SDL is used to handle input events in a cross-platform manner. The initialization, event handling, and cleanup code are abstracted, making it easier to adapt the game for different platforms.

Cross-Platform Graphics Rendering

One of the most important aspects of game creation is graphics rendering, and portability can be facilitated by using cross-platform graphics APIs. Examples of cross-platform graphics APIs that work with multiple operating systems are Vulkan and OpenGL.

Example: Cross-Platform Graphics Rendering with OpenGL

```cpp
#include <GL/glew.h>
#include <GLFW/glfw3.h>

// Cross-platform graphics rendering using OpenGL and GLFW
class Renderer {
public:
    // Initialize GLFW and GLEW
    bool initialize() {
        if (!glfwInit()) {
            // Handle initialization error
            return false;
        }

        // Set GLFW options and create a window

        // Initialize GLEW
        glewExperimental = GL_TRUE;
        if (glewInit() != GLEW_OK) {
            // Handle GLEW initialization error
            return false;
        }

        return true;
    }

    // Render graphics
    void render() {
        // OpenGL rendering code
    }

    // Clean up resources
    void cleanup() {
        glfwTerminate();
    }
};
```

This example showcases the initialization of GLFW for window management and GLEW for OpenGL extensions. The rendering code can be adapted for different platforms without significant modifications.

Cross-Platform Sound and Audio

Cross-platform audio libraries guarantee consistent sounds across multiple platforms. Popular cross-platform audio API OpenAL offers capabilities including multi-channel audio and 3D spatialization.

Example: Cross-Platform Audio with OpenAL

```cpp
#include <AL/al.h>
#include <AL/alc.h>

// Cross-platform audio using OpenAL
class AudioManager {
public:
    // Initialize OpenAL
    bool initialize() {
        ALCdevice* device = alcOpenDevice(nullptr);
        if (!device) {
            // Handle device initialization error
            return false;
        }

        ALCcontext* context = alcCreateContext(device, nullptr);
        alcMakeContextCurrent(context);

        // Additional initialization code

        return true;
    }

    // Play audio
    void playSound(ALuint sound) {
        alSourcePlay(sound);
    }

    // Clean up resources
    void cleanup() {
        ALCcontext* context = alcGetCurrentContext();
```

```cpp
        ALCdevice* device = alcGetContextsDevice(context);

        alcMakeContextCurrent(nullptr);
        alcDestroyContext(context);
        alcCloseDevice(device);
    }
};
```

In this example, OpenAL is used to initialize audio devices, play sounds, and manage audio contexts. The abstraction provided by OpenAL allows for seamless integration into cross-platform game projects.

Cross-Platform Compilation and Build Systems

Using cross-platform build tools makes it easier to compile code across several platforms. With just one configuration, the flexible tool CMake creates build files tailored to each platform.

Example: CMakeLists.txt for Cross-Platform Compilation

```cmake
cmake_minimum_required(VERSION 3.15)
project(MyGame)

# Add source files
file(GLOB_RECURSE SOURCES src/*.cpp)

# Set executable target
add_executable(MyGame ${SOURCES})

# Include directories
target_include_directories(MyGame PRIVATE include)

# Link libraries (SDL, OpenGL, OpenAL, etc.)
target_link_libraries(MyGame PRIVATE SDL2 OpenGL OpenAL)

# Set C++ standard
```

```
set_property(TARGET MyGame PROPERTY CXX_STANDARD 11)
```

This **CMakeLists.txt** example demonstrates how to configure a project for cross-platform compilation. Include directories and linked libraries can be adjusted based on the target platforms.

In C++ game programming, cross-platform development entails utilizing cross-platform libraries, build tools, audio systems, and graphics APIs. Developers can produce games that function flawlessly across a variety of platforms by implementing these strategies. Examples utilizing SDL, OpenGL, OpenAL, and CMake were presented in this section to demonstrate how versatile these tools are for cross-platform programming.

Porting games across different platforms

One of the most difficult but important aspects of game creation is porting games to other platforms. We'll look at methods and approaches in this part for effectively translating C++ games to different hardware setups and operating systems.

Platform-Agnostic Code Design

A key component of making the porting process easier is writing code that is platform-agnostic. Through abstraction of platform-specific elements, developers can create a strong base that easily transitions between many contexts.

Example: Platform-Agnostic Input Handling

```cpp
// Platform-agnostic input handling
class InputHandler {
public:
    virtual void processInput() = 0;
```

```cpp
    // Additional platform-agnostic input methods
};

#ifdef _WIN32
// Windows-specific implementation
#include <Windows.h>

class WindowsInputHandler : public InputHandler {
public:
    void processInput() override {
        // Windows-specific input handling
    }
};
#endif

#ifdef __linux__
// Linux-specific implementation
#include <X11/Xlib.h>

class LinuxInputHandler : public InputHandler {
public:
    void processInput() override {
        // Linux-specific input handling
    }
};
#endif
```

In this example, the **InputHandler** class provides a platform-agnostic interface for processing input. Platform-specific implementations are then defined based on preprocessor directives.

Abstraction Layers for Graphics and Audio

Developers can design code that is consistent across platforms and can adjust to different rendering and audio APIs by using abstraction layers for graphics and audio.

Example: Abstraction Layer for Graphics Rendering

```cpp
// Abstraction layer for graphics rendering
class GraphicsRenderer {
public:
    virtual void render() = 0;
    // Additional platform-agnostic rendering methods
};


#ifdef _WIN32
// Windows-specific implementation
#include <d3d11.h>

class WindowsGraphicsRenderer : public GraphicsRenderer {
public:
    void render() override {
        // Windows-specific rendering using Direct3D
    }
};
#endif


#ifdef __linux__
// Linux-specific implementation
#include <GL/gl.h>

class LinuxGraphicsRenderer : public GraphicsRenderer {
public:
    void render() override {
        // Linux-specific rendering using OpenGL
    }
};
#endif
```

In this example, the **GraphicsRenderer** class defines a platform-agnostic rendering interface, with platform-specific implementations utilizing Direct3D on Windows and OpenGL on Linux.

Adapting Build Systems for Different Platforms

It is essential to modify build systems for various platforms in order to produce project files or scripts that are compatible with the build tools of each operating system.

Example: Platform-Specific CMake Configurations

```
cmake_minimum_required(VERSION 3.15)
project(MyGame)

file(GLOB_RECURSE SOURCES src/*.cpp)
add_executable(MyGame ${SOURCES})

target_include_directories(MyGame PRIVATE include)

#ifdef _WIN32
    target_link_libraries(MyGame PRIVATE Direct3D)
#endif

#ifdef __linux__
    target_link_libraries(MyGame PRIVATE OpenGL)
#endif
```

In this example, the CMake configuration includes platform-specific directives for linking libraries based on the target platform. Adjustments can be made to include other dependencies or configurations as needed.

Testing and Debugging on Target Platforms

To find and fix problems unique to each environment, extensive testing and debugging on target systems are necessary. Testing across many operating systems can be done via emulators, simulators, or real hardware.

Example: Platform-Specific Debugging

```
// Platform-specific debugging code
#ifdef _DEBUG
```

```cpp
#ifdef _WIN32
    #include <Windows.h>
    #define DEBUG_LOG(message) OutputDebugStringA(message)
#endif

#ifdef __linux__
    #include <iostream>
    #define DEBUG_LOG(message) std::cout << message
#endif
#endif

int main() {
    // Game logic

    // Debugging message
    DEBUG_LOG("Game initialized successfully!\n");

    return 0;
}
```

In this example, platform-specific debugging messages are defined based on preprocessor directives, allowing developers to receive relevant information during the debugging process.

C++ game porting to many platforms requires careful consideration of abstraction layers, platform-specific modifications, and design choices. Examples of platform-neutral code design, audio and graphic abstraction layers, customizing build systems, and testing/debugging techniques were given in this section. When you are porting your C++ game to other platforms, take into account the particular features and needs of each target environment.

Handling platform-specific features in C++

In order to optimize and improve the gaming experience for various operating systems and hardware configurations, handling platform-specific characteristics is essential. We'll look at methods for adding platform-specific functionality to C++ game programming in this part.

Detecting the Target Platform

Developers can modify the functionality of their games according to the unique characteristics and capabilities of the operating system by detecting the target platform during runtime.

Example: Runtime Platform Detection

```cpp
#include <iostream>

enum class Platform {
    Windows,
    Linux,
    MacOS,
    Unknown
};

Platform detectPlatform() {
#ifdef _WIN32
    return Platform::Windows;
#elif __linux__
    return Platform::Linux;
#elif __APPLE__
    return Platform::MacOS;
#else
    return Platform::Unknown;
#endif
}

int main() {
    Platform currentPlatform = detectPlatform();

    switch (currentPlatform) {
        case Platform::Windows:
            std::cout << "Running on Windows\n";
            // Windows-specific code
```

```cpp
            break;

        case Platform::Linux:
            std::cout << "Running on Linux\n";
            // Linux-specific code
            break;

        case Platform::MacOS:
            std::cout << "Running on MacOS\n";
            // MacOS-specific code
            break;

        case Platform::Unknown:
            std::cout << "Unknown platform\n";
            // Default behavior
            break;
    }

    // Common code for all platforms

    return 0;
}
```

In this example, the **detectPlatform** function determines the current operating system at runtime. Depending on the detected platform, specific code sections are executed.

Leveraging Platform-Specific APIs

Utilizing platform-specific APIs allows developers to access unique features and functionalities available on each platform.

Example: Windows-Specific API Usage

```cpp
#ifdef _WIN32
#include <Windows.h>
```

```cpp
void windowsSpecificFunction() {
    // Windows-specific code using native API
    MessageBox(nullptr, "Hello Windows!", "Platform-Specific
    Feature", MB_OK);
}
#endif

int main() {
    // Common code

#ifdef _WIN32
    windowsSpecificFunction();
#endif

    // Common code

    return 0;
}
```

In this example, a Windows-specific function is defined to showcase the usage of the native Windows API. Conditional compilation ensures that the function is only included when targeting the Windows platform.

Optimizing Graphics for Different GPUs

Optimizing graphics for different GPUs involves utilizing platform-specific graphics APIs and adjusting rendering techniques based on the capabilities of each graphics card.

Example: Adapting Rendering for DirectX and OpenGL

```cpp
#ifdef _WIN32
#include <d3d11.h>
void renderUsingDirectX() {
    // DirectX-specific rendering code
```

```
}
#endif

#ifdef __linux__
#include <GL/gl.h>
void renderUsingOpenGL() {
    // OpenGL-specific rendering code
}
#endif

int main() {
    // Common code

#ifdef _WIN32
    renderUsingDirectX();
#elif __linux__
    renderUsingOpenGL();
#endif

    // Common code

    return 0;
}
```

In this example, platform-specific rendering functions are defined for DirectX and OpenGL. The appropriate function is called based on the target platform.

Utilizing Platform-Specific Input Methods

Different platforms may have unique input methods, and adapting to these methods enhances the overall user experience.

Example: Adapting Input Handling for Windows and Linux

```
#ifdef _WIN32
#include <Windows.h>
```

```cpp
void handleWindowsInput() {
    // Windows-specific input handling
}
#endif

#ifdef __linux__
#include <X11/Xlib.h>
void handleLinuxInput() {
    // Linux-specific input handling
}
#endif

int main() {
    // Common code

#ifdef _WIN32
    handleWindowsInput();
#elif __linux__
    handleLinuxInput();
#endif

    // Common code

    return 0;
}
```

In this example, platform-specific input handling functions are defined for Windows and Linux. The appropriate function is called based on the target platform.

In C++ game development, handling platform-specific features necessitates a combination of runtime detection, using platform-specific APIs, and modifying code according to each platform's distinct features. The given examples demonstrate how to detect platforms at runtime, use platform-specific APIs, optimize graphics for various GPUs, and use platform-specific input techniques. Take into account the unique characteristics and specifications of your intended platforms as you apply these tactics to your game production.

Performance Optimization Techniques

Developing C++ games requires careful consideration of performance optimization to ensure responsiveness and fluid gameplay. We'll look at a number
of ways to improve your game's performance in this chapter.

Profiling and Benchmarking

Profiling and benchmarking help identify performance bottlenecks in your
code, allowing you to focus on optimizing the most critical parts of your game.

Example: Basic Profiling with chrono in C++

```cpp
#include <iostream>
#include <chrono>

void timeConsumingFunction() {
    // Simulating a time-consuming operation
    for (int i = 0; i < 1000000; ++i) {
        // Some computation
    }
}

int main() {
    auto start = std::chrono::high_resolution_clock::now();

    // Code to be profiled
    timeConsumingFunction();
```

```cpp
    auto end = std::chrono::high_resolution_clock::now();
    auto duration =
    std::chrono::duration_cast<std::chrono::microseconds>(end -
    start).count();

    std::cout << "Time taken by function: " << duration << "
    microseconds\n";

    return 0;
}
```

In this example, the **timeConsumingFunction** simulates a computationally expensive operation, and the **chrono** library is used to measure the time taken by the function.

Memory Management

Efficient memory management can significantly impact performance. Avoiding memory leaks and optimizing data structures contribute to better overall performance.

Example: Using std::vector Instead of Arrays

```cpp
 #include <vector>

 int main() {
     // Array
     int array[1000000];

     // Vector
     std::vector<int> vector(1000000);

     // Accessing elements
     array[0] = 1;
     vector[0] = 1;
```

```
        return 0;
    }
```

In this example, using **std::vector** provides dynamic resizing and better memory management compared to a fixed-size array.

Multithreading

Utilizing multithreading can improve performance by parallelizing tasks, especially in computationally intensive parts of your game.

Example: Basic Multithreading with std::thread in C++

```
#include <iostream>
#include <thread>

void parallelFunction(int threadID) {
    // Simulating parallel computation
    for (int i = 0; i < 1000000; ++i) {
        // Some computation
    }

    std::cout << "Thread " << threadID << " finished\n";
}

int main() {
    // Creating two threads
    std::thread thread1(parallelFunction, 1);
    std::thread thread2(parallelFunction, 2);

    // Joining threads
    thread1.join();
    thread2.join();

    return 0;
}
```

In this example, two threads are created to execute the **parallelFunction** concurrently, simulating parallel computation.

Optimizing Loops

Efficient loop structures can significantly impact performance. Minimizing loop iterations and utilizing loop unrolling are common optimization techniques.

Example: Loop Unrolling

```cpp
#include <iostream>
#include <vector>

// Original loop
void originalLoop(const std::vector<int>& data) {
    for (size_t i = 0; i < data.size(); ++i) {
        // Process each element in the loop
        std::cout << data[i] << " ";
    }
}

// Loop unrolling
void unrolledLoop(const std::vector<int>& data) {
    size_t i = 0;
    size_t size = data.size();

    // Process elements in multiples of 4
    for (; i < size - 3; i += 4) {
        std::cout << data[i] << " ";
        std::cout << data[i + 1] << " ";
        std::cout << data[i + 2] << " ";
        std::cout << data[i + 3] << " ";
    }

    // Process remaining elements
    for (; i < size; ++i) {
        std::cout << data[i] << " ";
    }
```

```cpp
}

int main() {
    std::vector<int> data(1000000, 42);

    // Original loop
    originalLoop(data);

    // Unrolled loop
    unrolledLoop(data);

    return 0;
}
```

In this example, the **unrolledLoop** function demonstrates loop unrolling, a technique that reduces loop overhead by processing multiple elements in each iteration.

In C++ game development, optimizing loop structures, multithreading, effective memory management, and profiling are all part of performance optimization. By making sure the game works smoothly, these strategies help to improve the overall gaming experience. Take into account the unique needs and features of your game when you apply these optimizations to your project.

Strategies for performance enhancement

In C++ development for games, performance optimization is an ongoing process that calls for a variety of tactics to maximize code execution. This section looks at many tactics and methods to improve your game's performance.

Data-Oriented Design

Data-oriented design focuses on organizing and accessing data in a way that maximizes CPU cache efficiency, reducing memory latency and improving performance.

Example: Structure of Arrays (SoA) vs. Array of Structures (AoS)

```cpp
#include <vector>
#include <chrono>

// Array of Structures (AoS)
struct ParticleAoS {
    float x, y, z;
    float velocity;
    float mass;
};

// Structure of Arrays (SoA)
struct ParticleSoA {
    std::vector<float> x;
    std::vector<float> y;
    std::vector<float> z;
    std::vector<float> velocity;
    std::vector<float> mass;
};

// Update particles using AoS
void updateParticlesAoS(std::vector<ParticleAoS>& particles) {
    for (auto& particle : particles) {
        particle.x += particle.velocity;
        particle.y += particle.velocity;
        particle.z += particle.velocity;
    }
}

// Update particles using SoA
void updateParticlesSoA(ParticleSoA& particles) {
    for (size_t i = 0; i < particles.x.size(); ++i) {
        particles.x[i] += particles.velocity[i];
        particles.y[i] += particles.velocity[i];
        particles.z[i] += particles.velocity[i];
    }
}

int main() {
```

```cpp
    // Initialize particles
    std::vector<ParticleAoS> particlesAoS(1000000);
    ParticleSoA particlesSoA;
    particlesSoA.x.resize(1000000);
    particlesSoA.y.resize(1000000);
    particlesSoA.z.resize(1000000);
    particlesSoA.velocity.resize(1000000);

    // Measure time taken by AoS
    auto startAoS = std::chrono::high_resolution_clock::now();
    updateParticlesAoS(particlesAoS);
    auto endAoS = std::chrono::high_resolution_clock::now();
    auto durationAoS =
    std::chrono::duration_cast<std::chrono::microseconds>(endAoS -
    startAoS).count();

    // Measure time taken by SoA
    auto startSoA = std::chrono::high_resolution_clock::now();
    updateParticlesSoA(particlesSoA);
    auto endSoA = std::chrono::high_resolution_clock::now();
    auto durationSoA =
    std::chrono::duration_cast<std::chrono::microseconds>(endSoA -
    startSoA).count();

    // Output results
    std::cout << "Time taken by AoS: " << durationAoS << "
    microseconds\n";
    std::cout << "Time taken by SoA: " << durationSoA << "
    microseconds\n";

    return 0;
}
```

In this example, the structure of arrays (SoA) approach improves cache efficiency by storing particle properties in separate arrays, reducing memory access latency.

SIMD (Single Instruction, Multiple Data) Optimization

SIMD instructions allow parallel processing of multiple data elements in a single instruction, enhancing computational efficiency.

Example: SIMD Optimization with Intel Intrinsics

```cpp
#include <iostream>
#include <immintrin.h>

void vectorAddSIMD(float* a, float* b, float* result, int size) {
    for (int i = 0; i < size; i += 8) {
        __m256 vecA = _mm256_loadu_ps(&a[i]);
        __m256 vecB = _mm256_loadu_ps(&b[i]);
        __m256 vecResult = _mm256_add_ps(vecA, vecB);
        _mm256_storeu_ps(&result[i], vecResult);
    }
}

int main() {
    const int size = 1000000;

    // Initialize arrays
    float* arrayA = new float[size];
    float* arrayB = new float[size];
    float* result = new float[size];

    // Populate arrays with data

    // Measure time taken by SIMD vector addition
    auto start = std::chrono::high_resolution_clock::now();
    vectorAddSIMD(arrayA, arrayB, result, size);
    auto end = std::chrono::high_resolution_clock::now();
    auto duration =
    std::chrono::duration_cast<std::chrono::microseconds>(end -
    start).count();

    std::cout << "Time taken by SIMD vector addition: " <<
    duration << " microseconds\n";

    // Clean up
```

```
        delete[] arrayA;
        delete[] arrayB;
        delete[] result;

        return 0;
    }
```

In this example, SIMD optimization is achieved using Intel Intrinsics to perform vector addition on arrays of floating-point numbers.

Minimizing Branching

Reducing branching in code can enhance performance by improving branch prediction accuracy.

Example: Minimizing Branching with Conditional Move

```
    #include <iostream>
    #include <chrono>

    int conditionalMove(int a, int b, bool condition) {
        // Traditional branching
        if (condition) {
            return a;
        } else {
            return b;
        }

        // Using conditional move
        // return condition ? a : b;
    }

    int main() {
        const int iterations = 1000000;
        bool condition = true;

        // Measure time taken by traditional branching
```

```cpp
    auto startBranching =
    std::chrono::high_resolution_clock::now();
    for (int i = 0; i < iterations; ++i) {
        int result = conditionalMove(i, i * 2, condition);
    }
    auto endBranching = std::chrono::high_resolution_clock::now();
    auto durationBranching =
    std::chrono::duration_cast<std::chrono::microseconds>(endBranching
    - startBranching).count();

    // Measure time taken by conditional move
    auto startCondMove = std::chrono::high_resolution_clock::now();
    for (int i = 0; i < iterations; ++i) {
        int result = (condition) ? i : i * 2;
    }
    auto endCondMove = std::chrono::high_resolution_clock::now();
    auto durationCondMove =
    std::chrono::duration_cast<std::chrono::microseconds>(endCondMove
    - startCondMove).count();

    std::cout << "Time taken by traditional branching: " <<
    durationBranching << " microseconds\n";
    std::cout << "Time taken by conditional move: " <<
    durationCondMove << " microseconds\n";

    return 0;
}
```

In this example, the impact of traditional branching versus conditional move on performance is measured using a simple conditional operation.

Using SIMD optimization, reducing branching, and implementing data-oriented design are three ways to improve performance in C++ game programming. These tactics make the game more responsive and efficient when paired with benchmarking and profiling. Take into account the unique needs and features of your game as you apply these strategies to your project.

References

***C++ Primer* by Stanley B. Lippman, Josée Lajoie, and Barbara E. Moo**

This book provides a comprehensive introduction to C++ programming, covering essential concepts and features that are foundational for game development.

***Effective C++: 55 Specific Ways to Improve Your Programs and Designs* by Scott Meyers**

Scott Meyers offers practical advice and best practices for writing efficient and maintainable C++ code, making it a valuable resource for game developers aiming to enhance their programming skills.

***Game Programming Patterns* by Robert Nystrom**

This book focuses on design patterns specifically tailored for game development. It provides insights into creating scalable and robust game architectures.

***C++ Concurrency in Action* by Anthony Williams**

For developers interested in optimizing game performance through multi-threading and concurrent programming, this book offers in-depth coverage of C++ concurrency features.

Optimized C++: Proven Techniques for Heightened Performance by Kurt Guntheroth

Kurt Guntheroth explores advanced techniques for optimizing C++ code, which can be invaluable for game developers aiming to enhance the performance of their applications.

Real-Time Rendering, Fourth Edition by Tomas Akenine-Möller, Eric Haines, Naty Hoffman, Angelo Pesce, and Michał Iwanicki

This authoritative reference on real-time rendering covers fundamental principles and techniques crucial for creating visually compelling and performant graphics in games.

Programming Game AI by Example by Mat Buckland

Mat Buckland's book provides practical examples and insights into implementing artificial intelligence in games, contributing to the scalability and robustness of game applications.

C++ Game Development By Example by Siddharth Shekar

This book walks through practical examples of C++ game development, offering hands-on experience and guidance for building scalable and robust gaming applications.

Modern C++ Design: Generic Programming and Design Patterns Applied" by Andrei Alexandrescu

Andrei Alexandrescu's book explores advanced C++ design concepts, including generic programming and design patterns, which can be valuable for game developers seeking to create flexible and scalable architectures.

Introduction to 3D Game Programming with DirectX 12 by Frank D. Luna

For those focusing on DirectX for game development, Frank D. Luna's book provides a comprehensive introduction to 3D game programming, emphasizing scalable and efficient techniques.

About the Author

E. Jarrel is a college teacher who teaches computer programming courses . He has been writing programs since he was 15 years old. Jarrel currently focuses on writing software that addresses inefficiencies in education and brings the benefits of open source software to the field of education. In his spare time he enjoys climbing mountains and spending time with his family.

Also by Jarrel E.

Python Mastery Unleashed: Advanced Programming Techniques

Python Mastery Unleashed: Advanced Programming Techniques is a comprehensive guide to mastering advanced programming techniques in Python. Designed for seasoned Python developers and aspiring programmers alike, this book offers a comprehensive understanding of the advanced programming techniques used by experienced Python developers to build complex systems and applications.

From Zero to Java Hero: Master The Art of Java Programming

From Zero to Java Hero: Master the Art of Programming is a comprehensive guide designed to empower aspiring programmers with the knowledge and skills needed to excel in the world of Java development. This powerful book offers a transformative journey from a complete novice to a proficient Java developer. Are you ready to embark on a journey that will elevate your programming skills to new heights? From Zero to Java Hero is the ultimate guide for individuals with little to no coding experience who want to unlock the full potential of Java programming. Whether you're a student, a career changer, or someone with a passion for technology, this book will equip you with the tools to become a Java hero.

Python for Data Science: A Practical Approach to Machine Learning

Dive into the world of data science with Python for Data Science: A Practical Approach to Machine Learning. This comprehensive guide is meticulously crafted to provide you with the knowledge and skills necessary to excel in the ever-evolving field of data science. Authored by a seasoned writer who understands the nuances of the craft, this book is a masterpiece in itself, delivering a deep dive into the realm of Python and its application in data science. The book's primary focus is on machine learning, making it an invaluable resource for those seeking to harness the power of data to make informed decisions. In Python for Data Science, you'll find a well-structured and organized approach to learning Python, with an emphasis on its real-world applications. The book presents the subject matter with clarity and precision, ensuring that every concept is explained in a coherent and logical manner.